THE RESTLESS RELIGIOUS

THE *Restless*
RELIGIOUS

BY ROBERT W. GLEASON, S. J.

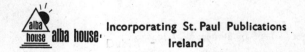

alba house · Incorporating St. Paul Publications
Ireland

Imprimatur: † Joannes McCormack, *Ordinarius*
                    Mullingar
              April 26th, 1969

The *Nihil Obstat* and the *Imprimatur* are official declarations that a book
or pamphlet is free of doctrinal or moral error. No implication is contained
therein that those who have granted the *Nihil Obstat* and the *Imprimatur*
agree with the opinions expressed.

Printed in Ireland
by the Society of St. Paul,
Ballykeeran, Athlone

▟ AUTHOR'S PREFACE

THIS BOOK IS dedicated to the countless religious men and women across the world who dialogued with me on the importance of the religious life. They have generously shared with me their experiences, their insights, their concerns, and their criticisms of abuses. For well over a decade I have participated in workshops, institutes, and conferences on this topic, in America, Europe, and the Orient. Members of over two hundred religious congregations from a score of national and cultural backgrounds have helped in the formulation of the material presented here. Aware of the crisis that confronts religious life today, many have urged that I publish the text of these informal conferences in the hope that this book may help others better to formulate their current problems. The tentative character of much expressed here, its informality, its fragmentary approach, reflects its origin, in *en famille* dialogue. I have deliberately retained the questions most often posed to point up the exchange of viewpoints that took place in actual dialogue.

Not all religious, obviously, will agree with the viewpoints expressed here nor will the experience of all support every aspect of the analyses of present difficulties. A full-scale theology of the religious life has yet to be attempted, and this book carries no such pretension. It hopes to be a modest intrafamilial exposition of what religious from widely differing backgrounds have thought and said about the problems that confront our religious family today. All that is valuable in this book I ascribe to the generous men and women who spoke out frankly, sometimes bluntly, but always in love, about the very real dangers that threaten the continued existence in the Church of a form of life that has served her nobly for many centuries.

It is my hope and my loving conviction that the book will soon be rendered obsolete, having stimulated more comprehensive and more scientific studies, theological and sociological, of this important subject.

┏┛ PREFACE

THE WINDS of change are blowing across the plains of the Church. In some instances these winds are gentle, warm and nudging; in others their velocity and intensity have reached almost hurricane force.

The results of these changes have been equally divergent. In this preface to Father Gleason's new book, I would confine my remarks to that vast plain in the Church's life known as religious life.

Christians have embraced the religious life from the earliest days of Christ's Church. The dedication and commitment of individuals to Christ in a total and unique giving of self has been one of the most visible signs of holiness within the Church. The Holy Spirit has continued to breathe holiness upon religious over the centuries.

The unique role of religious in the Church's life and their influence within the world community is without question. Much has changed in the world and in the Church. Scarcely a human value or endeavor remains concealed from the searching, questioning mind of modern man. Perhaps one of the more valuable roles of today's religious would be to serve the Church and the world as a sign of stability and perseverance.

A sense of stability is ennobling, not limiting. The mature religious can lend that sense of value to twentieth century Christianity which many feel lacking. One perceives a frustration among Christians because of seemingly conflicting forces. On the one hand all are anxious to let the Good News of Christ serve as the basis for modern Christian living; on the other traditional forms of Christian life and practice are being abandoned as irrelevant.

Many are questioning the place of religious in today's Church. The question is not whether to retain religious life as a distinct form within the Church, but rather to search out more fully the more valuable role of religious in our times. Perhaps so much uncertainty and restlessness persist because religious of past years have not questioned their own roles, purposes and goals. To question is not to dissent; to adapt is not to disobey.

I commend Father Gleason for crystallizing for us many of the contemporary problems affecting not only the entire Church but also individual religious. His concern for the individual is central to the progression of his treatise.

While many problems have surfaced in our decade the Church's future is not one of despair or bleakness. Over-reaction to emerging problems serves only to compound the search for expressions of a more intense, personal witness of Christ among God's People. Not everyone will share the author's analysis of the problems nor his recommended solutions. But his willingness and openness in meeting the problems with the perspective of a mature and sensitive religious will help create an atmosphere of dialogue among all religious.

A sense of mature responsibility in religious life may possibly be the key factor in finding solutions to current problems and bringing true interior peace in the midst of unrest. The Second Vatican Council began a worldwide quest for maturity within the whole Church. Religious must be equally attuned to the promptings of the Holy Spirit, particularly as each grows more mature in the likeness of Christ. The author aptly portrays this Christian maturity in his eloquent chapters.

As religious we must be sincerely honest with ourselves

and with one another. We must create an atmosphere of freedom that will elicit a fuller sense of individual as well as community worth. We cannot be threatened or fearful of change when such change truly reflects the best interests of the religious, the religious community and the Church.

Religious life holds out to the world community a source of hope and comfort as well as a symbol of challenge. By pursuing a life of unique holiness the religious will bring that needed balance between Christian apathy and hyperactivity. Holiness will always be relevant. Christ sent the Holy Spirit to be with us until the end of the world in order to foster that personal union with Christ. While many religious groups continue to discuss the forms of their active life their commitment to holiness must be ever intensified. The holiness of religious life will bring that stability which so many search for.

Religious share in a special way the challenge of finding new ways to bring Christ to men. Most religious communities are engaged in special works. What a contribution these communities could make if they were to experiment with new forms of the apostolate and thereby serve the community of men with new ways of leading souls to the Father through Christ.

While no book ever answers all questions or solves all problems we feel that Father Gleason has made a significant contribution in clarifying many of the root issues and in stimulating discussion around the complex and pressing problems of today's religious.

Most Rev. Aloysius J. Willinger,
C.Ss.R., D.D.

⊞ CONTENTS

ONE · MALAISE IN RELIGIOUS LIFE

A CRUCIAL MALAISE is manifest in the Church today, especially in the microcosm of the Church: religious life. We are in an age of renewal; religious customs are being re-evaluated. What is sometimes called *ressourcement* is going on; Christian thinkers are going back to the sources, making historical investigations, and many concepts, once blithely taken for granted, are now being challenged. There are signs that all is not well. Some of these signs have evidently been visible to the highest authorities of the Church: has there not been a Council called which discussed them?

When Pope John called the Council, it was to renewal, to free and open discussion. Still, there was disagreement at the Council: different emphases upon different problems by different sides. The same will be true in any re-evaluation of the permanent values attached to the religious life. But the spirit calling us to make this evaluation is one of mutual dialogue, mutual openness, mutual charity, under the influence of a non-partisan Holy Spirit.

Religious are fortunate in the renewed interest in the religious life now being shown throughout the world: this has provoked fundamental and potentially profitable debate. All the attitudes, opinions, and suggestions put forward will not be accepted permanently, yet they have created areas of reflection and discussion. These will help. Religious should be particularly grateful that their intellectual situation has changed—and changed remarkably over the last thirty years. Today we see astute theologians entering the area of ascetical theology, reserved, in the past, for

1

textbook theologians. Spirituality, once the fringe of theology—though every once in a while some expert wrote a small article, a reflection, a theological insight—now has theologians: Karl Rahner, George Thils, and others, giving religious problems their effort, their historical and speculative research, and even their genius.

Religious Orders are also in a favorable situation from another point of view: they are no longer isolated when they deal with questions of ascetical, mystical, and religious importance. No longer is the discipline of theology the only science clarifying these problems. We have fellow disciplines. Sociologists, with all the technical skills, use their insights, their discoveries, to help analyze the spiritual attitudes to be assumed in this crisis of religious life. Psychologists are making important contributions—the most important of the last twenty years. They help us to an in-depth analysis; they evaluate religious attitudes, differentiating the authentic from the pseudo. We only hope these contributions will continue, and become even more widely publicized.

Then, too, the prophetic words of the literary artist have aided religious of this generation. We see analyses, in the concrete, in contemporary literatures, of psychological and spiritual attitudes. These have often imaged truth in a fashion less vague than abstract analysis. We need not necessarily agree with all these analyses, but we cannot be unprovoked by *The Nun's Story* or *Two Nuns* or *I Leap over the Wall*. We have also had novels on the priestly vocation, its splendor and its decadence. First of these is Graham Greene's *The Power and The Glory*. *No Small Thing* and *Vessel of Dishonor* also described the areas of conflict in a priestly vocation, human and dramatic in perspective. The number of books on the religious life makes a new focus of discussion evident, an importance specific to our generation. The schema for religious promulgated in Vatican II, *Perfectae Caritatis*, gives new perspectives too.

These new signs of vitality are counterbalanced by certain critical signs of malaise with regard to the religous life. The question is raised today: is this particular form of life within the Church obsolete? This question is raised seriously, not, as one might expect, by outsiders, but by religious themselves. Of course it is possible that a form of life which served the Church nobly at one period should become obsolete in another. Among the signs of malaise, some are extremely serious. Others indicate a general, widespread change. The general point of view of a generation influenced by two brutal wars—and a number of "minor" ones—is necessarily less complacent than the one preceding it.

In discussing these challenges, I hope to focus sharply on the validity—or invalidity—of these signs. In describing them, I do not mean to approve—some, in fact, seem to me logically incompatible. But each is evidence of the need for discussion, evaluation, reflection, and openness to the Spirit, to see what the Spirit may suggest, may approve of, in this apparent opposition to religious life.

The happiest sign of the malaise we observe is the quantity of books openly discussing what, thirty years ago, would not have been even comfortably thought. The sociologist Houtart has recently offered us a book on the *Challenge to Change*. He makes an analysis of the attitudes behind the difficulties in the contemporary religious life of the Church. He also suggests that these challenges and these difficulties pave new avenues for the quest: how shall we find the will of the Lord now?

In de Lubac's book on the Church, one chapter is dedicated to the filial and loyal criticism that may and should be directed to the Church. Here, again, we enter a controversy. For some think filial loyalty demands not only submission, but total intellectual docility: all flaws and blemishes, even major ones, of a Church not yet of eschatological glory, should be ignored, simply and totally ignored. Others insist the call of loyalty is to *full* truth. Since the Church need never fear truth, we should proclaim, most frankly and candidly, everything we find of critical import —even, indeed, describe in detail the unattractive blemishes of a beloved Mother. These two attitudes de Lubac tries to resolve intellectually; he does a splendid job. We have, too, Michael Novak's *The Open Church*, and Daniel Callahan's *Honesty in the Church*. That these books can be written, and published, by loyal churchmen and devoted sons, is more than progressive; it is revolutionary.

True, on the other side, there have been movements, well-intentioned no doubt, gently, if firmly, to check these sources of debate. One must expect that there would be in a dialogue of this sort differences of opinion; we can usually credit all sides with good faith. The type of anticlericalism noted throughout the world, not unfamiliar in Europe, is becoming more familiarly American. This too indicates a certain malaise, an undercurrent of discontent beyond the structure of religious life. It affects our catechetical approach. Our kerygmatic and liturgical approach may also be due for considerable re-thinking.

Besides these scattered indications, we have—now familiar to all—the "New Breed." It poses some problems for teachers and religious. It is difficult for us to read ourselves into their psychological and cultural situations. In analyzing the objections of this group, we are sometimes startled and surprised to note the vigor of their way of posing problems and their insistence on a point of view. Whether or not we agree, it is existentially there; if we want to be honest, we have at least to recognize it. The questioning attitude so common today, at times seeming to leave no subject or truth untouched, is new to an older age group; yet this questioning may be the voice of the Spirit. The Spirit is not restricted to speaking through the mouths of those who have passed forty or ninety. St. Benedict advised elders to listen to the young. The group we sometimes label the New Breed has been characterized as indocile—perhaps truly so! It is intellectually somewhat indocile: it prefers explanations to statements or orders, and it is characterized particularly by youth's impatience with what it considers formalism, particularly an older generation's formalism. Admittedly, an intellectual formulation of one generation is inadequate for another. If knowledge is a fact, so is its advance. The intellectual approaches and solutions elaborated in the thirteenth century by a genial St. Thomas need not be the absolute and complete solution to the problems of today's sophomore. Our era is a time of rapid change. Everything is experimental; all is new. In the New Breed, we observe willingness to experiment and openness to the untried. We see also a startling honesty, an honesty not always flattering and frequently outspoken, if not blunt.

But the sign of malaise disturbing most people today, perhaps because it is measurable and tangible, is the failure of vocations to the religious life. This may be a result of a recent emphasis—one badly needed—on the "nobility and dignity of the vocation of marriage and the lay apostolate." In emphasizing this, we have perhaps failed to show consecrated virginity or the sacerdotal vocation or the religious vocation as a noble, if not a superior vocation. We must face the fact that in some areas of the world, there seem to be very few vocations to the religious life. In some areas, these vocations, when they exist, are restricted to certain types of religious life. Interestingly enough, often the contemplative vocation seems to do very well, in numbers, whereas the mixed life seems less attractive to modern youth—except, perhaps, for those Orders directly devoted to the care of the poor or to the missionary apostolate.

Many question today the meaningfulness of the religious vocation. Many are distressed by so many religious leaving their Orders, and those often the most generous and talented. If this is true, it should give us pause; it should also give us pause if it is true that the brilliant leave and the mediocre stay. While it may be the will of God that religious carry on their work with pedestrian talent, occasionally, it is hoped, He may raise up a prophet in our midst. If religious life cannot make sociological room for the prophetic voice, it may be doomed to a kind of *aurea mediocritas*.

Religious today claim that they are not leaving religious life because it is difficult or sacrificial; they are leaving because they are frustrated. They consider themselves betrayed as human beings in the intellectual order, the spiritual order, and the psychological order. This is a serious charge. A contributing factor to this malaise is the fact of cultural telescoping. The youth of today are about four generations removed from the middle-aged, culturally and sociologically. With the rapid increase of communications and the growth of technology, things happen more quickly, fashions change overnight, ideas spread like wildfire. We cannot even keep up with the spiritually restless Joneses. As a result, there will be defined conflicts: youth will challenge age, each trying the respect of the other.

A different approach to the same problems among sincere people who happen to belong to one age group or the other age group is just as manifest. Age, of course, cannot always be measured by a chronometer. Some people in their eighties are still radical, and far more progressive than the young liberal who becomes the middle-aged conservative, a graybeard by forty. Some older people can entertain problems, even explore undeveloped areas to find new vistas, assimilating young ideas more easily than the young. Certainly this was so of Pope John. His extraordinary human response to the Holy Spirit led him to see the problems of our age, although he was not a gifted intellectual in the analytic and theological order.

There is also obvious today a certain re-questioning of values taken for granted for centuries. Especially does one note a questioning of the traditional exposition of the evangelical counsels as means to perfection. The vows of poverty, chastity, and obedience need a reformulation, and there are many theologians working on this. It is not easy. It may be easy to repeat explanations traditionally given as to the value of these vows, but it is not so easy to answer the theological and psychological objections urged against them. There is, for instance, the widespread questioning of the value of celibacy. In one European country, many seminarians insist that they have the right to marry. It is quite common in that country for ordained priests to marry and to invite their clerical friends to the reception. Sometimes many clergy attend these marriages, canonically invalid. This questioning of the value of celibacy means that one must re-think the authentic values contained therein. We must provide an exposition of celibacy to fit into our culture, while still retaining its permanent validity.

There are also certain signs of dissatisfaction which break forth in a *sub rosa* and at times even in public rebellion. One hears of pray-in strikes, quasi-disobedience or "holy" disobedience to legitimately constituted juridical authority. Holy disobedience was a topic recently much discussed at a national meeting of theologians. This topic needs a great deal of theoretical elaboration before it can be made fully intelligible, much less applicable to a concrete situation. There have also been sociological studies, asking religious what they thought of their spiritual, intellectual, psychological formation, and asking seminarians what they thought of theirs. Curiously, these studies have often not been published.

All of these elements and many others contribute to a widespread feeling that all is not entirely well in religious life. The specific areas of criticism most discussed bear largely upon the intellectual life, the spiritual life, and the psychological life. In exposing these criticisms, I am not endorsing them. These criticisms are to be modified according to the concrete situation. The problems encountered in the U.S.A. are not the problems encountered in Spain. There are variations according to the particular tradition of each religious group. The problems of Carmel today are not likely to be the problems of the Dominicans or of the

Jesuits. There are problems that are common to one sex: nuns and Sisters have certain viewpoints; priests and Brothers have different ones. The problems in and of the contemplative life are not the problems in and of the active life. Some problems vary according to special spiritual traditions: some groups have a spiritual tradition which is easily adaptable, adjustable, mobile, open; others have a tradition which is more antique—in the best sense of the word—implying a tradition that has survived many centuries and survived them well. All these differences modify the problems as they occur in each group. Now is it possible to isolate some of the problematic areas, some of the neuralgic points for discussion?

If some of the charges against religious life are true, then it is clearly the unconditioned will of God that we try to cope with them. If, for example, it is true that religious life as it is lived today in the concrete, existential, historical, real order produces infantile personalities, then religious Orders ought seriously to consider what can be done to modify the structure and the sociological conditions of the group. It is obviously not the will of God that we should continue producing infants when He has invited us to adulthood. On the intellectual plane, there is visible today a distress—at times an anguish—almost a despair, among young religious, which would not have been common in another generation. Our educational apostolate has expanded; we have become more professional-minded, more diversified in our apostolate. As a result there is bound to be a certain area of conflict between the intellectual and the spiritual. Unless we work out a spirituality of intellectuality which allows everything to fall into its proper place, we will experience conflict. Even if we had evolved such a spirituality in the abstract and theoretical order, it would be difficult to bring it into operation in the precise delimited concrete situation. If I am a scientist, my students ask today why I should be ordained at all. In what sense does one function as a priest and as a scientist? Is not one's major preoccupation as a scientist the intellectual order? Can not one do just as good a job as a layman? If we reply, "I work as a priest on weekends in a direct apostolate," they reply, "Yes, but in other words you have saved this for that time which is your free time. Really what you should be doing if you are a good scientist is devoting that weekend to science, and not taking away time from your research." A conflict can thus develop between the intellectual and the spiritual.

The intellectual area also poses a problem which is sometimes phrased like this: Is it actually possible to be an intellectual in a highly organized and highly structured religious group? Would it not be spiritually preferable to choose the lay vocation where, unhampered by the restrictions of authority, obedience, decisions handed down from on high, one could pursue one's work in a personal fashion with personal research? Is it not true that in any highly structured institutional group, such as the religious life, one is bound to have eternal Galileos? Is it true that the intellectual cannot breathe freely in the type of climate formed by our modern institutionalized religious life? On the other hand, we may also ask: If religious life is a reflection of the Church, is she not bound to be the native homeland of truth and intellectuality, if she fulfills her own vocation?

The second intellectual problem often heard is: Is it true that religious by and large tend to have a fondness for predigested solutions to everything? Is it true that they have a native tendency to avoid launching out into the deep in any direction? Do they stay on the surface? Is there any profundity to religious exploration of the crucial problems of modern life? Do religious feel deeply touched by them, or do they feel alienated from modern civilization? Are they able to produce—are they given the requisite intellectual conditions to produce anything in the way of depth at all? Are they educated to a certain prefabricated approach to life in which everything will fall into its proper place if only they accept a thirteenth-century schema of reality?

The Christian intellectual today also poses the question whether or not religious, in their tradition, have not a certain worship for antiquarian formulae. Are they subjected to a naïve traditionalism in training which tends to make them feel that the Christian tradition began in the thirteenth century and ended there? Can religious speak to the modern world? Do they have their fingers on the pulse? In other words, is an intellectual vocation to the religious life viable in the atmosphere of contemporary religious life?

Another question often posed in the intellectual area is this: What is the respect for individual talent given by an institution which has large corporate works? It must continue to keep these afloat (although some of them perhaps might be abandoned without damage to the institution), but at what cost to the individual? What is the amount of deliberate or half-deliberate destruction of individual talent in this group? Is there a preference for a talent of a certain golden mediocrity? If so, religious ought deliberately to advertise that they seek mediocrity in candidates. Most are not prepared to do so. The intellectual who poses this question also asks the question whether the genius can exist in contemporary religious life—not as some kind of isolated phenomenon, but as a real individual in a day-by-day social process and structure, a genius alive and productive.

Religious Orders have made great strides here. Thirty years ago it would have been uncommon for an individual to enter the structure of religious life and announce that he or she wanted to be an artist. Today we have come closer to respecting this viewpoint. Do religious, however, have such rigidly predefined molds to their structure that the concrete uniqueness of a God-given vocation cannot be respected? Although this charge may have less validity in some places than in others, it seems true. Do they have real openness toward adjustment in the apostolate, or is their approach obsolete? There are many who feel that the works of mercy and of charity, so glowingly characteristic of the Church since her very beginning, such as the operation of hospitals and orphanages, can now be handed over to a secular society which performs such functions more competently. Religious would then be left free for other works. The more fundamental question is: Are religious Orders willing enough and mobile enough to debate the area of the apostolate, or has the structured religious approach to life frozen them in traditional categories? It is certainly true that groups of religious founded to teach the poor, today teach the rich. Could these groups not broaden their apostolate? In a sense, every communication of God's words is a "teaching." Do religious also manifest a certain disregard for the Lord of truth, regard God simply as goodness and fail to realize that He is also substantial Truth? Do they have a contempt for truth, abstract truth? Do they manifest an instrumentalization of truth and research? In a highly structured religious group, would one be told what truth he is supposed to find after he has completed his analyses?

Would one be directed ahead of time as to what truth should be, rather than be given sufficient freedom to find it? In support of this charge, we are told to look at what goes on in the concrete real order. A man or a priest, told to get a professional degree, is promptly put into another discipline. A man is told to get a Ph.D. When he has his "union card," every condition is set down so that he cannot use his research techniques or his knowledge. That, if universally true, would hardly be tolerable. It would indicate an unhealthy anti-intellectualism, a certain instrumentalization of the value of truth itself.

As a group, are religious educated to be perceptive thinkers or are they educated to a kind of trade-school professionalism? Do they learn a number of non-liberal disciplines, let us say, canon law or theology, and having learned them, become strangers to that open, inquiring, investigating mind they claim to want to produce in their students? Are religious in any sense "out of touch" with concrete reality because of their formation? Are they kept in cotton batting so that even the brightest cannot respond to real problems because they cannot feel the concrete, existential nuances of a problem, because they approach it in too protected a way, or under conditions too oppressive, whether these be philosophical or theological? These are some of the questions in the intellectual area put to religious life today. If all are to be answered negatively, the charge of betrayal of the intellectual order would be true.

The spiritual order poses questions as well. It is strange to realize that some believe a form of life approved by the Church as a means to perfection implies a kind of spiritual betrayal. Yet this is sometimes charged. Truth requires that it be discussed.

Some of the problems of the spiritual formation of religious concern the vows; others concern the simple routine of daily life. Let us consider one—and an obvious one today —the question of the vow of poverty. At times, religious are asked: "You take the vow of poverty, but in what sense do you ever experience the effects of poverty?" This question is being put quite bluntly to the religious groups ascribing to themselves the most severe poverty in the Church. In certain forms of cloistered life, Superiors are sometimes told by the professed that their way of life is not viable because it is not genuinely *poor!* That is a question to be discussed in another chapter.

The other problem often discussed is the problem of self-sacrifice versus self-fulfillment. Generation upon generation of Christians was brought up with the idea of the cross, a reality in the Christian life, a sign of the whole religious reality. Sacrifice is necessary. It is an expression of love. There are "fulfillments" beyond the natural. Yet the youth of today, agreeing with all that, asks this: In what sense am I going to be genuinely fulfilled as a human being in this group? God Almighty did not call me to this group simply to be an example of sacrifice. Am I not also to be personally fulfilled in the unique, unrepeatable vocation He gave to me? If a religious Order cannot promise "yes" to that, then the vocation will be lost. It is, of course, very difficult for anyone to promise someone what the Providence of God has in store for him. Moreover, occasional natural frustrations often mean ultimate supernatural fulfillment. Youth, however, with its ardor and generosity, has a certain impatience with long-continued frustration.

The third question often posed today is the reconciliation of the apostolate with the interior life. This is posed even in the strictest contemplative Orders of the Church. It is a very urgent question today because all have to support themselves. Even Trappists and Carmelites and Poor Clares have to eat. They are, of course, also supposed to work. The tension always characteristic of the mixed life is now part of the contemplative life. Work has a tendency to absorb all our energy. How, then, do we reconcile the contemplative with the active life? Where do we make the decisions? Are there clear boundary lines or clear theoretical guidelines laid down, or have religious come to an idolatry of activity? Have we a theology of work? A theology of leisure?

Then what about the authentic Christian value of that private prayer once so much emphasized in religious life? Some believe this type of prayer urges one to pray for personal sanctification, to meditate upon his own vices and the Lord's virtues, to strive to imitate the latter and repress the former, to grow in the expansion of the divine life planted in us by baptism—only to result in a kind of spiritual selfishness. It does not, they say, lead so easily to personal sanctification as communal prayer, public prayer, the service of the liturgy. We are even told that it is characteristic of conservative religious groups to have little feeling for the official prayer of the Church. Rather, they have stepped into a little, private cul-de-sac, a private ism. Some religious groups feel that it really does not matter what one does: pick up stones or water dried sticks, teach class, preach a sermon, hear confessions. One occupation is as good as the other as long as it has been commanded by "obedience." This type of excessive supernaturalism, desert-spirituality, appalls the modern mind. God is not only the Creator of invisible realities; He also created visible ones. This world, too, has a divine importance. It is not easy to suggest or command a watering of dried sticks to solve problems.

At other times, religious are accused of excessive naturalism. Cost what it may, they are supposed to produce the external results: get this class taught, get that work done. Whether one prays does not matter. One assumes, somehow, that in the twenty-fifth hour they will get prayer in; they will fulfill quietly, tranquilly, and peacefully, in the presence of God, all those aspirations for which they came to this kind of life. In the other twenty-four hours: *Do the job!* That kind of naturalism, basically an adoration of material, external achievement, results in a type of evacuation of the cross of Christ. Achievement is adored at the price of esteem for prayer, virtue, and charity. The interior apostolate, prayer, and the genuinely *supernatural* aspects of even the most apostolic of vocations are often ignored or condemned—as simply not practical.

European thinkers have their own difficulties with American spiritual formation: they call it "bourgeois mentality." They maintain that old established religious Orders, and even some of the younger, have produced religious of middle-class vices and virtues, neither of great depth. American religious, they say, are not particularly bad, nor are they particularly good. They are those lukewarm Christians who will be vomited out of the Lord's mouth because all that they have is a bourgeois mentality structured according to an official form of "spiritual life." American fondness for counting the number of communicants, and the number of confessions, may be called a spiritual materialism, they add.

We must also touch on the question most prominent in the last twenty years: freedom versus docility. By freedom I mean the freedom of the children of God, not license, the abuse of freedom. Is this freedom actually compatible with the necessary structure of obedience and docility encouraged by the religious life? That is a problem I will discuss at some length in Chapter Three.

It is also suggested that the spirituality given to most religious is based on half truths, thus, half lies. Clichés are common, clichés which will not stand up under any theological scrutiny. Such a cliché is: "A Superior's will is God's will." In a sense, of course, it is. And in a sense, of course, it could not be; a Superior is hardly divine.

There is also a widespread resentment against religious today because they seem to show a massive disengagement from the great spiritual crises of our own time. One is asked: "What have they done by way of manifesting burning concern for the great social issues of the day? How did they lead in racial struggles? How far did they lead in civil rights, social justice? Are they reduced to a state of religious life that has no cutting edge? Are they concerned only with private morality? Do they conceive the kingdom of God as 'no smoking, no gambling, no card-playing, and no to a few items of sexual mores'?"

Are they also notable for hardness of heart? This is a strange question to ask people vowed to virginity, a form of perfect love. Whenever that question is asked, one thinks of that long list of wicked acts Paul puts down in Romans; he concludes with what may be the wickedest, to be *sine affectione*. Are religious without human warmth, tenderness, affection, and expansiveness? Are they without *humanitas*? This charge points to a failure to understand the Christian virtue of detachment, a virtue caricatured to produce a pre-Christian stoicism, a Druidic mentality, if not plain stupidity. The virtue of detachment has certainly been caricatured at times. Let us by all means be *attached* to something, to someone, before learning, through love and selflessness, the stark difficulty of what it means to be detached.

Every authentic virtue can have its counterfeits. So, in the religious life, witness to the authentic voice of a Christian virtue can be fake, phony. If so, religious will not witness to Christ, the good Man, drawing all men to Himself through His love.

In the third order, the psychological, one observes many new, interesting, sometimes contradictory charges launched against the ancient institution of religious life. First, it is suggested, religious life is a kind of institutionalized nursery, a kindergarten to keep men infantile, dependent upon their fathers, their Superiors. Religious, it is said, cannot feel the anguish of human existence; how can they, protected as they are from the radically personal commitments any human being makes. Decisions are made for the religious. But why one should be free from the anguish of existence merely because he has to obey another's decisions is not clear. Those decisions can even cause a modicum of anguish. Is it true that the ordinary religious is taught to show too much dependence? It is characteristic of an adult to have a certain independence in judgment, action, decision, in accepting the reality of himself in society. Does the normal religious show infantile dependence? In deeper, more personal questions, more radical issues, is he able to decide for himself? Does the religious show to the world an inability to give and receive real love? Because he is not married, does not have sexual expression, is the religious unable to come to adulthood, unable to give warm, human affection, or receive it easily and freely from another, within moral limits? If true, this would mean that a form of life approved in the Church leads to immaturity. Is that God's will? Docile and obedient, do religious manifest a certain disengagement, apathy, in place of Christian commitment? Certain household words in some religious Orders corroborate this. When one hears often, if not too loudly, such slogans as "Don't get involved," "Don't go out on a limb," "You'll get hurt," one may conclude that the supreme Christian value is to "play it safe." That is not an absolute. We should remember Christ and His cross.

Another criticism, sometimes put in a very forceful way, says religious manifest what St. Paul condemned as the *prudentia carnis,* the prudence of the flesh. Prudence of the flesh, a kind of emasculated Christianity, will, under difficult circumstances, not speak out for truth or principle or value because "prudence" forbids it. But Christian prudence is a forceful virtue; they who understand it are not emasculated by it.

Is there a psychological immaturity manifested in religious life today—a psychological insecurity due to the formation process? Psychological insecurity often provokes envy, resentment, lack of generosity, coziness, carefulness. Is there a common inability among religious to confront the human person and his problems? Is deviousness fostered to lessen friction? Does the attempt to preserve peace in religious life result in hypocrisies, if not lies? Is education in religious groups a teaching by fear rather than by love, educating the individual by marshalling all his neuroses, insisting on reprisals rather than illumination, or identifying a Superior's dictates with those of the Holy Spirit? Is there a kind of indoctrination substituted for deeply personal formation? Does a kind of ritualism replace commitment?

It is suggested by some that religious life fosters a form of psychological insecurity. If the individual is not made to feel he is loved and wanted, he becomes insecure; he then behaves badly. A difficulty many young people suggest today is this: religious are characterized by inability to confront persons openly as persons. If, for example, a religious disagrees with a Superior, why cannot the two talk as human beings, as is done in the business world, in the social world, as persons meeting to discuss a difference?

It is often asserted that the authoritarianism prevalent in religious life makes it look like a totalitarian, highly secular form of government. This type of government is destined to break the human spirit, to crush it, to submit it to authority, without disagreement, rebellion, personal initiative. Another difficulty suggested is this: the religious attitudes which ought to be deeply personal are often only stereotypes formed by an education based upon fear. "I do this or I will get it"; "I do this or I will be gotten at." Thus neurotic tendencies, fears, guilt feelings, are marshalled behind directives in a fashion that produces a robot, not a person.

It is also argued that religious formation is a training too external and ritualistic. Instead of deep, personal, pneumatic Christian commitments—commitments that arise from the very depths of a person's essential self—there are only pietistic, formalistic, externalistic responses contradicting the genuine Christian impulse.

At times there seems to be a lack of honesty among religious. No one seems to fully trust or know anyone else in the group; while outright lies are not common, half truths or evasions are automatic, common, and prompt.

The individuality given to the institute by God is not cultivated but repressed, it is said. God gives to this particular individual special talents, but they are not developed and caused to grow for the apostolate. Rather they are repressed and pushed into another form of activity.

Another charge often made is that religious are characterized by a sheer lack of humanity. They show none of the humanity and benignity of God, none of the warmth, the witness to Christ's charity; they display rather a neurotic defense against involvement with others, a sign of immaturity.

At times, it is said, they seem to show an immunity to the sufferings of others—an immunity created by their own rather bovine attitudes.

It is often charged that there is little living at the depths, little generosity, because this has been smothered by creature comforts, petty routine, and a life protected against the new, the shocking, the real.

It is said that an historical, existential notion of vocation is ignored, and ideals are aimed at that provoke self-hatred rather than self-love. That *authentic*, Christian self-love commanded by Christ and necessary for love of others and God is checked, it is claimed, by "humility."

Another defect noted by the modern mind in its attack upon the religious life is that love of power, that traffic in other human souls which the modern mind considers worse than slavery, black or white, but which some claim is indigenous to religious life.

Still another difficulty is that religious sometimes act as though they were exempt from the Ten Commandments or the natural law. It is suggested they seem to believe that the end justifies the means, that they are exempt, for example, from justice toward those they employ, or toward fellow religious, or from truth or integrity or honesty.

It is commonly said that there is manifest among reli-

gious a fear of interpersonal relations. Religious come together without knowing one another, live together without
loving one another, and die without caring for one another.
A fear of life, with all its dangers and threats and invitations, is also implicit in this charge. That materialism char-
acterizing the modern world, and against which religious
battle, is at times charged against them. They are, it is said,
preoccupied with comfort, with recreation.

The charges brought against the vows are that they
deform the human personality instead of bringing it to its
completion. Obedience, it is said, gives man a freedom from
responsibility, a freedom from initiative, and renders him
passive. Poverty can create a lazy monk. One's needs are
taken care of, at least in the essentials, and sometimes in the
non-essentials. Chastity can be presented as freedom from
the necessity of loving and as the sacrifice of human adulthood, in other words, as nothing but a return to a pre-adult
narcissistic adolescence, a preoccupation with self as an
isolated individual.

These charges can be met, and they must be met in the
intellectual order. The answers are not easy. We have to
reflect as to why the questions are being asked in the first
place. Some say that if a committed Christian *saw* clearly
the splendor and the glory of the priestly vocation and the
religious vocation, he or she would not be posing such
questions. But often they are coming from our most Christian youth! That is the characteristic change notable today.
It is not said that the religious life is not a worthwhile life
because it implies sacrifices. The problem is being posed in
another fashion. Whether we accept the way it is posed or
not, we have to confront it. The problem is being posed
thus: "Is religious life actually valid as a form of life lead-

ing to perfection *in the concrete, historical situation of today?* Or does it, no matter what it proclaims in the *abstract, ideal* order, produce, in the concrete, malformed personalities, neurotics, people incapable of doing what normal, dedicated Christians in the lay world would do and achieve for the Kingdom of God?" If the question is posed that way, we have to discover the deep wellsprings of this malaise. What have we religious done, what limitations do we have, what deficiencies do we have, what departures have we tolerated from the ideals of our founder that have provoked this malaise?

THE PRACTICAL APPROACH

QUESTION. "Is it better to be obedient at the cost of diminishing effectiveness for the apostolate, or to seek to develop one's gifts for the Church outside obedience?"

ANSWER. If a man could fulfill God's call to him personally and individually and at the same time develop his potentialities as a religious and as a person, then he would fulfill himself more perfectly under obedience.

If, however, to remain in a religious group implies a loss of his sanity, of personal integrity, of his most Christian convictions, a diminution of his personal talents, then to remain there would be less perfect. I do not think that the picture ever presents itself in such a white or black fashion. What we have to work out is some kind of concrete solution to each case, and the case is rarely that clear-cut.

QUESTION. "Is it true to say without further distinction that when I obey the will of my Superior, unless it be a sinful command, I obey the will of God?"

ANSWER. That is a very simple way of stating an extremely complex theological truth which requires careful application in the concrete. If a Superior were to command something which is not sinful, but utterly irrational, stupid, and harmful to the apostolate, for the good of the apostolate and the good of the religious group I must make certain gentle protests and eventually less gentle protests. I must appeal to ever higher and higher authority. These problems are not easily solved. The unrest which the modern mind feels in tackling them is felt precisely because all is not black or white. It is not that some are all perfect and others are all wrong, that some have all the right insights and others all the wrong convictions. Truth often lies in a tension, a polarity between two truths which are both partial. We have to make a synthesis between the two. The Church is supreme over the State in religious matters. Yes. It is also true that the State has a valid autonomous existence in the secular order. It is both truths which we must bring together, somehow, in a synthesis. This is what is happening today in many ascetical problems. We have to restate, with nuances, our principles and also listen to the objections which come to us in the hope of making ourselves intelligible to modern youth. There is a great problem in the fact that different areas of the world express a dissatisfaction with the image of the religious in contemporary life.

QUESTION. "What is meant by a caricature of the vows?"

ANSWER. When I used that expression, I meant an approach to the norm which deforms their original meaning. For example, a monk can—because his vow of poverty gives him security—show less of the intense drive, energy, virtuous ambition than a businessman. On the other hand, if he fully understands his vow of poverty, the vow should give him freedom for a zeal that is *greater* than any privately motivated zeal. This deformation is also possible with the vow of virginity. Virginity is not a freedom from human love. On the contrary, no one is fit to take that vow who is not capable of human love, not sufficiently adult to love. Virginity is a consecration to Jesus Christ which universalizes love in a face-to-face confrontation with Jesus Christ. If vows are explained positively and lived to their full, youth might not have so many objections to religious vows.

It is true that the religious does not have imposed on him the sacrifices imposed on married couples which break down egotism and render men more susceptible to charity. Religious can become self-enclosed at times by a misuse of virginity. If interpreted as a dehumanization of the personality, virginity could create old bachelors without warmth or openness. Virginity should give a freedom for a more universal, a more intense form of love. The same is true of obedience. It channels and guides initiative, but it is not supposed to create a power structure which destroys initiative or renders one passive. The religious has no vocation to passivity. He has a vocation to controlled initiative. The initiative comes from me; the control comes from the Superior. Thus we can achieve more things in common and I can receive direction from the Holy Spirit through juridically established and defined channels.

If obedience is so interpreted or practiced that the individual ends up as a passive agent, something to be shoved here and there, it can not appeal to the modern world, which respects the value of personal dignity and freedom, or to a Christian.

QUESTION. "Does it not seem that the Church and religious Orders have been to a large extent dominated by juridical categories essentially legal and Roman, preoccupied by the universal to the extent that the individual has been submerged?"

ANSWER. Yes. And the insights of modern psychology and existential philosophy and modern living and culture as a whole, have brought the individual to the fore so strongly that he now refuses to be treated as one of an amorphous mass or a juridical cog. This is providential for us. God did not bring to any religious group one more unit of ten. He brought these concrete individuals who are irreplaceable historically for the rest of time. We have to respect that individuality, in all its irreplaceability, its uniqueness. We have not always done so. It is obviously easier to handle groups than individuals. At times, religious groups have failed to appreciate the uniqueness of a vocation. The Council is now opening new approaches and new insights. Those truths developed by existentialism, e.g., a feeling for the person, for subjectivity, for development, for process, will have to be integrated into our way of dealing with religious life. It is only in the last thirty years that we have initiated theological reflection on what we have been living over the centuries.

QUESTION. "Is there a correlation between intellectuality in the religious life and defection from it?"

ANSWER. It has become increasingly impossible to frustrate brilliant people and keep them happy. They will not accept frustration in this modern world. If a particular group, or a particular House, is such that there is not permitted free expansion of individual talents, it will not long endure. If individuals are systematically frustrated, they will end up psychologically deformed. More often, they will leave religious life for their peace of soul, and to live the Christian commitment. If a genius is given by God to a group, God intended that the Order deal with—a genius. We have not had a full tradition of treating each one according to his personal differential. At times the frustrated individual is treated as though he were disobedient. Intellectual frustration is not intended by God. Occasionally, God permits a rare vocation to be almost totally frustrated, but the prudent man would not—not being the Holy Spirit—dare to impose that vocation on individuals under his care. The modern world feels very intensely the reality of created values. It is convinced that these values are genuine: this world has genuine value; intelligence has genuine value. These are not things to be condemned. Modern man feels legitimately frustrated if a situation arises in which his abilities cannot be realized. There is also manifest today a certain lack of patience among religious, perhaps because of the accelerated tempo of modern life. P. T. de Chardin could wait five, ten, fifteen years; modern youth is not convinced that at this period in history, God is calling them to wait that long, especially when the only thing impeding progress seems to be a lack of understanding of the fundamental spirit of the religious way of life on the part of religious.

QUESTION. "Does not the spirit of poverty call on us to open up new apostolates so as to have new areas of work more in keeping with poverty?"

ANSWER. We ought to explore with great openness the possibility of shifting and expanding the apostolate. The question has certainly arisen as to whether or not we must be irrevocably committed to past apostolates. Are there not new forms of apostolate? Perhaps the large corporate works to which we are committed need not swallow up and gorge down every individual in the Order. There are new apostolates in the Church. Who would have thought of the Little Brothers of Charles de Foucauld and their work a few years ago? We ought to show the adaptability that is a sign of life. We ought not to close our eyes to any situation where a Christian can bear witness even though it may not be in a traditional form or pattern.

With regard to the question of poverty, we have to face the fact that this is a question which is related to our apostolate. All too often religious expand in such widespread directions, spread themselves so thin, that money is just not available for excellence. Where there is a question of allocation of money, we should have community discussion; whether we need three millions dollars for a campus center or whether a library is more needed should be a discussion of the whole group.

QUESTION. "If religious life is a deeper living of the commitment of baptism, and if the Church is reshaping her life, can we rethink these problems apart from the rethinking going on in the Church?"

ANSWER. We should not attempt that. If we solve problems in isolation from the mind and will of the Church, we are going in a bad direction. The Church herself in re-thinking and in reformulating her consciousness of her existence today, has issued an invitation to religious to re-think their patterns of life. In some cases, she has issued explicit directions, even though leaving a great deal of freedom to individual Orders to formulate their traditions against the background of their history and vocation.

QUESTION. "Have not Sisters shown a lack of leadership in the Church?"

ANSWER. They sometimes show a lack of initiative. How many, when the Ecumenical Council of the Church was called, asked to be represented? They have contributed to the Church a work which could not be done by any other group, with a generosity which provokes the admiration of the Church, but they did not ask to be heard at the Council. They retired to feminine passivity and waited to see what male votes would decide.

QUESTION. "Since the problems are so advanced and the actualization of a solution is so far behind, how can we avoid disaster?"

ANSWER. If we had open discussion, we would create an interim period during which we might find solutions before disaster occurs. And by open discussion, I do not mean the kind of discussion in which a Superior says, "You may dis-cuss this and arrive at that conclusion." I refer to honest discussion. Very often, the fact that a group has expressed its opinion enables it to accept tranquilly a directive op-posed to that opinion, feeling that the air has been cleared. Women religious are engaging in discussion today more than men are. They have accepted the idea of community discussion of problems. In most places where it is done, even where there is a wide diversity of theoretical approach to the ascetical life or the apostolate or to personal development, even where there is a very wide disparity in the intellectual formation, the spiritual formation, the age group, one observes a kind of ferment of active or dynamic peace. We should pull difficulties out from under the rug and ask, "Where do we go from here?" If we do that, we can avoid disaster. If people see signs of progress, they are not likely to give way to despair.

⊞ TWO · PROBLEM AREAS

IN THE PREVIOUS chapter, I outlined some of the alleged difficulties which may lead to a triple betrayal of the religious family. Whether or not these charges are true has not yet been discussed in detail. If they are, then we could say, at least, that they produce difficulties which will result in inauthentic living. In this chapter, now, I will attempt a clarification by noting other questions and problem areas. We ought not overspecify solutions at this stage. If we merely pose the problems in a new perspective, we have already arrived at some approach to a solution. One of the greatest difficulties in the history of theological and philosophical problems is this: one cannot solve a problem correctly until one *poses* it correctly. And one cannot pose it correctly until it is put in a completely new perspective; this demands breaking traditional categories of thought and reaction. If religious were to pool their shared concerns, there might come about a sharing of insight, a definition of common areas of agreement and disagreement. Problem areas can then be explored more in detail. Different human beings have different experiences and react differently to them, categorize them, formulate them differently. We should not imply bad faith to anyone who disagrees with us. We should rather reflect on their position in trying to come to some kind of dynamic solution.

There will always be a tension in facing these crucial issues: to think the past is wrong and the present is right—everything old is bad; everything new, good—and *vice versa* is not mature. Religious usually agree on the most general principles. All could agree, for example, that we

31

should do good and avoid evil. We have, however, eventually to arrive at more specific statements. But we have to come there rather cautiously because of the crisis we are experiencing—a crisis in the common usage of that term. It is obvious from the malaise already described that there are certain problems, something—at least in appearance—not right in the religious family which, like the Church, is both human and divine.

In another sense, today shows a crisis situation: we have to take a stance; the moment calls for a thoughtful response to difficulties. In still a third sense, we are in a state of crisis. For everyone engaged, at this particular moment in history, in the exploration of religious life, this is a *kairos* moment, an unrepeatable moment in salvation history. One cannot find, twenty years from now, the solution proper to today, apply it then, and rest then, content. The processes of history are irreversible; the elected moments in salvation history must be responded to promptly. If we do not respond at the moment, the opportunity is gone; only history remains. So we must attempt to balance factors. It is an old scholastic adage that virtue stands in the middle—an adage not quite true, of course, of the prime virtue, charity; but it can stand as a norm for us. Rarely does the truth lie fully on one side or on the other. When one really touches the truth, as one sees truth in God, in whom apparently opposed attributes are actually identical, one incorporates both complementary factors or aspects of the truth. Unless religious share some kind of common, concrete experience, their knowledge of solutions, even though correct, may remain notional, a knowledge with little amplification or resonance in man's concrete historical existence. There is little advantage to that kind of abstract knowledge. To solve concrete problems, we need an *idée-force* which does something, generates something, has some active influence in the personality. If not, knowledge is no more than conceptual; and if knowledge is not in some sense evaluative, it does not act as a motive force in life. It is not operative. When it is a question of good, of value, we need a quite different kind of knowledge; we need a knowledge somehow touching the concrete, backed up by experience, connatural with its object. This kind of knowledge is sometimes called knowledge by connaturality, knowledge specific to areas where values exist. A conceptualized formulation of solutions to religious problems will not work, because it can be accepted conceptually; yet, when it touches action, it can submit to a strange reformulation almost *contrary* to the original insight. There can be a sudden readjustment of conceptual patterns so that egotism dominates the conceptual patterns and then, in effect, the knowledge is valueless.

Therefore, what religious need today is a corporate effort. They must pool common experience. Out of experience may come some tentative openings toward a solution of these complex and difficult questions—questions doubly complex because they are also the most theoretical in all theology. It is infinitely easier to teach the Trinity than to teach ascetical theology. In asceticism, we are dealing with problems of morality, psychology, dogmatic theology, the history of theology, and many parallel sciences, such as sociology. The questions posed in the last chapter are highly complex, highly elaborate. We have not come even to the proper formulation of some of them. This area is a "science of the concrete," if even that is possible.

Laymen often ask religious whether the recent Council has had any effect on their lives as religious. In many cases the laity poses questions openly to religious congregations. Sometimes this interest on the part of the laity is taken in good part; sometimes it causes resentment. "How dare these people, who have no experience of our tradition, ask us these questions and expect to receive an answer? What do they know about it? What are their motives? Why do they do it?" On the other side, these same questions provoke a certain amount of eyebrow-lifting: "How did these people ever manage to find just that neuralgic spot to touch?"

It also comes as a surprise to many religious that some religious and some laymen suggest a formal effort at renewal through the use of methods common to business and politics, for example, polling the members of the religious congregation. Yet this suggestion is quite practical and in no way destructive of religious spirit. It is simply a way of gathering information. Any professional sociologist could poll a congregation, but it is not a common practice to poll religious for their viewpoints. It seems to be a common and profitable practice in secular organizations, such as business groups concerned with making money more efficiently— banks, institutions of that sort—but in the area of the sacred, where tradition plays so large and important a rôle, and where ideals and objectives are more important than making money, I do not know of many scientific efforts of this kind. As a result, one often notes an attitude of profound discouragement on the part of some religious. They query whether their congregation has really any sincere desire to update. We could have asked the question about the Council itself. How can one tell if we are unwilling or unable to make formal studies to determine these matters? How can one even know the convictions of the group if one is unwilling to explore scientifically their convictions?

Families and friends of religious are often astonished at the use or abuse made of authority in religious congregations and ask for an explanation of its nature. Often we religious cannot give a very satisfactory response. Although we have clearly proved the Church to be an organization gifted with authority by God, and this authority legitimate, we have not explained this authority, theoretically, enough. Exploration by either Scripture experts or theologians into the precise nature of sacred authority, its evolution, its ultimate divine meaning, the meaning of its symbols in the Old and the New Testament, is rare. Recently we have begun to explore, but we cannot blame anyone who does not have, today, a theological understanding of, or an evolved theology of authority: it does not exist.

Psychologists and sociologists can be of great help in these areas.

Curiously, religious Orders have many brilliantly trained psychologists and sociologists, well able to do exactly what we would hope, yet they are rarely, if ever, asked to help. No doubt they are overworked; the tests may be difficult to evaluate—but all tests are. How do people manage in other areas? I do think it would be very helpful if religious experts would devote their free time, let us say, their recreation, to study the reaction to authority as based upon the Gospel, Christ's teaching.

Many religious simply assume that government must be autocratic. From the more recent papal statements, it would seem that democratic processes are part of the natural law; if so, the modifications that religious would have to make in a highly organized group, a group officially monarchic, are considerable. If what the popes have stated are really natural-law truths, we ought to reflect upon the present state of religious authority. Such reflection would, however, be difficult to carry out within the usual religious tradition.

It is clear that if religious congregations are to update, they must have clearly defined processes by which they pool the experience of *all* the group. Hit-and-miss methods are unpractical.

Yet formal channels, structured ways for doing this, are rare in religious life. I am not sure that there is not a kind of built-in check even where such procedures exist according to the letter of the law of the Institute.

It would also be very profitable for religious congregations to make scientific studies as to what draws young men or women to their congregation and what causes some to leave, and some to stay.

Some declining congregations today would have to answer "nothing" to the first question. Others, more successful, answer, "The Holy Spirit." Others might say, "This type of work, that type of work." To questions such as these, one gets an enormous, astonishing, and delightful variety of answers.

What persuades some to remain in the congregation while so many leave? Those remain who are better balanced, those who have a psychological, spiritual, intellectual equilibrium which fits them to meet all the diverse circumstances, good and bad, of their life. That would be at least one *possible* answer. Is it always the correct one?

There are few studies about those who leave. The few are not easily gotten at: one was hidden in the depths of a vault it took two keys to open. Yet it would be profitable, interesting, to find out why people leave who came to religious life with great gifts and with great generosity. Most religious groups do not start with the worst; they are selective and they look for people with talent, with some kind of personal gifts to give to the service of the apostolate. Often, they apply a number of newly devised psychological examinations; still, a great many religious do leave. It is essential to religious Orders to know frankly why they leave, even if answers shatter illusions. Putting aside insults and bitterness, one could evaluate the responses.

It has been suggested that one of the major causes why religious leave is assignment to work unsuitable to their talents. If so, more effort should be made to consult the individual before making an assignment. At present, in many groups, there is no consultation, or only formal consultation, even when the Institute imposes this. However somewhat more effort is made today, necessarily, because money has been spent in training subjects, to respect individual talents. If these talents fall into well defined categories—a Ph.D. in chemistry, *summa cum laude*—it is likely that the religious will be put into administration or in chemistry, or in something related to chemistry; that is to say, what a Superior thinks is related to chemistry: inorganic, physical . . . He may even have to teach physics or mathematics. All are sciences.

Many problems, of assignment as well as of other categories, arise from the fact that religious congregations have grown so large and assumed such diverse work. Most religious congregations began as a small group of men or women gathered about a leader, a man or woman with certain special insights. In the early days, before they were large, it was easy to maintain the fundamental orientation the founder or foundress had in mind. But as the group grew larger, it inevitably grew more structured, less dependent on insight, and more on law, form, rule.

Through their growth into larger organizations, religious Orders experience the tensions and difficulties already pointed up. The Church herself, for example, is partly human, partly divine. As the continuation of Christ Incarnate in time and space, she has certain divine attributes; she is transcendent to, but also immanent in history, in this world, this civilization. On the human side, she is represented by men, governed by men, under the direction of the Holy Spirit. Hence, she is subject to many of the human difficulties which occur in any secular institution. As soon as any group is formed, someone is going to be the leader and someone is going to be the follower. Immediately one has the question of authority and all the subsidiary effects of freedom versus authority. What is happening today in religious life is a thorough questioning of many procedures, apostolates, values which have been accepted for centuries as incorporating and embodying the fundamental insights of the founder or foundress. From a few basic ideas a congregation moves to a constitution, to an Institute, to rules, to customs. These tend to become more and more identified with the "spirit" of the Order or congregation, although in fact the founder may have had little or nothing to say about them. He or she might in fact repudiate many of them were he or she alive today. A great problem inevitably confronts religious Orders as to how to communicate the founder's insight to the present-day religious. We define concretely what the insight meant; we spell it out. Some founders did not want to do this at all; they maintained, "You have the Holy Spirit in you!" And that is true. Christ did not substitute a new law for the old law. The Old Testament was not abrogated in order to produce a New Testament. The Old Law was not substituted for by a New Law, but by a principle of life, the Holy Spirit, who is supposed to guide us. But since the Holy Spirit operates differently in different people, and since smaller men have a great love for the concrete, for clarity, a desire to know exactly what the law permits and what the law forbids, religious usually produce constitutions, customs and laws. As a result, the insight may become very obscure; the law may, in fact, betray the original insight. This happens, not out of ill will or malice, but because moral insight is a rare gift of the Spirit, and a small or ignorant or uninformed mind cannot always open up to the length and breadth of insight unless the Holy Spirit assists.

What a religious group should aim to do is to open up to each novice the total insight of the founder. Often this is not successful. There is an immanent tendency to substitute a kind of ritual performance; one insures that the ritualized performance goes on by the use of religious authority. Instead of an inner illumination of intelligence, the individual experiences indoctrination, brainwashing. That indoctrination is directed toward the best ends possible, but it is still an indoctrination program'. Religious must be very careful that they do not end up with an "Animal Farm," even though the characteristics of that farm might be, in some deviant form, a reflection of the original insight. Today's young religious are questioning many rules that may or may not be part of the real traditions of the group. Where the traditional rules, procedures, style of life, long determined and accepted, which shored up a religious' psychological and intellectual security are subjected to constant questioning, the individual is likely to be subject to tensions which threaten his inner security,

Religious institutions are clearly in a state of transition.

This should not upset or disturb us: it is an invitation from the Holy Spirit to provoke an honest, open response to the changing situation. But a transitional period involves certain dangers of which we should be aware; if we are open-minded and honest, we see the possibilities of dangers and difficulties. We should not opt for inanity and insist that all must be honey and milk because our "founder" was a saint. Our Church was founded by Jesus Christ, and it experiences transitional periods.

Christianity is involved in a dialectic. It involves a transcendent reality which is embodied in history and carried on by human persons. This provides the fundamental conflict, the conflict of event versus institution. The Christ event is the Church. Still we have a visible institutional Church, which has an externalized appearance, walls, and a history, as well as people, subjects, rulers. In the beginnings of any religious family, we observe the same situation. The founder was a prophetic personality who drew around him a group responding fervently to the "event." What attracted the first group of companions was the new religious insight, and a personality. The main focus of life and of orientation was the unrepeatable insight of an unrepeatable person. As time goes on, the primary insights of the founder receive sharper definition by virtue of repeated clarification. They may be genuinely incarnated in a multitude of works, ideas, sentiments, maxims, writings, a whole style of life. On the other hand, they can also be obscured. The main objectives and aims of the congregation can be lost sight of in the multitude of "clarifications." An Order founded to be most poor can become almost rich. The same process which affects the group with the passage of centuries can affect the individual religious in the course of his life span. Having entered to absorb the spirit and purpose of the founder, one can gradually shift his emphasis from this to more natural satisfaction—the satisfaction of one's natural abilities, abilities for work, ability to develop policies, to exercise one's personal apostolate. Religious life can satisfy not only the religious' desire to incorporate publicly and incarnate personally the insight of the founder, but also the desire that he receive the satisfaction of basic drives for experience, self-expression, scholarship, productivity.

Such a human complex of motivation implies certain obvious dangers. An individual religious may gradually move from the position of the original insight to one in which the original insight is almost obliterated by natural motivation. A religious motivation can deteriorate so that the original insight cannot possibly function with the new type of motivation. It is stifled. It is destroyed. A man may enter religious life in order to be a humble, docile religious. Having been appointed Superior for six years, and then going on for another six, or eight, or nine, or ten, or eleven, or twelve, or twenty, or twenty-five, his viewpoint may change considerably. Undoubtedly that man was prompted at first to dedicate his extraordinary and recognized talents for administration, to developing the will of the religious community. It can happen that the original insight gradually fades and a kind of "king mentality" arises: the motivation is now to "hold on to my power—at all costs." This is not unusual in the history of the Church or of religious Orders. We shall not comment on the present century, but it has happened in the past; if it happened in the past, it can happen again. "He who forgets the past," said Santayana, "is doomed to repeat it."

There is also the possibility that organizational

hypertrophy will result in bureaucracy. Because the bureaucrat can fulfill certain positions easily without "rocking the boat" or conceiving new ideas, he may become established in a position in which natural motivations, quite remote from or even opposed to the original motivation, suffice. One also observes a type of peculiar, unhappy, political alliance: "You give me this. I will give you that." Religious life occasionally produces cliques, begetting, in the spiritual order, their like. A certain type of Superior, strangely enough, may tend to produce the same type, even in the generation after. When that happens, one suspects that a natural motivation has taken dominance. There can arise a certain *hubris* in virtue of which, with great naïveté, one's immediate goal is identified with the goal of the Deity. How can He think differently? This type of simple vanity, at times tolerable, becomes intolerable when it is effectively divorced fom the founder's peculiar insight. At times we observe, as a kind of occupational hazard, a spiritual duplicity deemed necessary to prevent the emergence to full consciousness of the entire gamut of motivation. That type of game can work against not only the spiritual, but also against the psychological health of the one who indulges in it. This has been noted in the Church itself. In certain periods of history, she has manifested a form of politics unsuited to authentic religious life. One should not too easily identify one's particular motivation with the voice of the Holy Spirit.

Large religious institutions are also subject to "Parkinson's Law." Administration in religious life can become so complicated that one despairs of being able to get through channels to change anything. It can lead to a remoteness of the leader from those doing the actual work, so that he who

makes the decisions about the work may not have the
remotest idea about what he is deciding upon after its
passage through the enormously complicated maze of administrative channels. When that occurs, we behold a com-
plication of legalism and bureaucracy. There is bureaucracy
within the Church, and there is bureaucracy within religious orders. Bureaucracy serves a good purpose in insuring
law and order, but it is also subject to temptations of
rigidity and lack of imagination. Its service also tends to
attract less inspired members of the group. Moreover,
today's religious do not take easily to bureaucratic ways of
thinking and acting. The bureaucrat naturally tends to
emphasize the importance of the *status quo* and to look
askance at experimentation. He tends to overemphasize the
goals of the institution, or what he understands as its goals,
whereas today's religious prefer to consider the needs of the
individual. Most religious are willing to sacrifice a certain
amount of their individual preferences and talents to corporate goals, but they object to being turned into mere
instruments for the goals which the bureaucrat may decide
best suited to the inspiration of the Institute.

It is natural for the bureaucrat to accept direction from
above and to expect that decisions will be made at the top
echelon, whereas today's youth are more accustomed to
discussion, grass-roots initiative, and teamwork. The excessive emphasis that some administrators put on administrative status in a religious group sits ill with today's youth,
who prefer to give their allegiance to competence rather
than to position. Competence is the key word to youth
today: they are not particularly impressed by position or
authority unless those holding position display competence.
They expect a voice in decision-making in those areas in

which they actually work. Often this irritates the bureau-cratic mind; it is less orderly, less impersonal, and some-times seems an unjustified intrusion into what he considers his sphere, i.e., decision-making. Often, too, the young reli-gious insists upon the right of the individual to fulfill his talents in tasks not classical in the group, e.g., a religious in a teaching Order wishes to function.as an artist. The admin-istrative mind often fails to see how that contributes to the goal of the group or the institution. The administration should decide upon the needs of the institution, and then decide how best to employ its subjects. We must admit and reflect on these conflicts of viewpoint if we are going to cope with them. Initiative should normally not come from the top; initiative is supposed to come from the bottom. As a distinguished cleric said, "There never have been any ideas that originated in Rome and there shouldn't be. They should come from *us*, and Rome should judge us." With her bi-millennium wisdom and experience, her understanding of how to separate creative elements from destructive ones, the Church can judge. But if the administrative process gets too far removed from the troops, a lack of initiative results. Is any democratization of the structure of religious life possible? Can the least one still get to the top one? As St. Benedict said, the last little monk who entered should always be asked his opinion. Strangely enough, even though only sixteen, right off the farm, he, by native intelligence, by God's speaking to him, by his recent arrival from a concrete reality, may have something to say to assembled age and wisdom. This would be an excellent procedure to restore to religious life.

These dangers inevitably confront religious groups once they are past their first few years. They should not dismay us, yet we should be aware of them. It is for these reasons that we are called always to renewal. *Ecclesia semper reformanda* applies also to each religious family.

QUESTION. "Do not the structures of present-day religious life tend to produce an immature personality?"

ANSWER. Religious life *need* not destroy personality. Certain outmoded forms of institutional organization, certain attitudes of religious are less conducive to the formation of an adult personality, but these are not necessarily part of the fundamental structure of religious life.

QUESTION. "Should we look at these structures and discuss them openly and make such adjustments as the situation calls for?"

ANSWER. Certainly.

QUESTION. "Is power not used despotically at certain times in the religious life?"

ANSWER. It would be naïve to deny that it is. However, law has incorporated certain rights for priests and for religious. These rights are embodied in law, and it is the will of the Church that they be observed. Those who do not observe them are in disobedience to the Church, *whatsoever position they hold.* The Pope is above canon law, but *no one* else is.

QUESTION. "Does prudence demand that we do nothing about this?"

ANSWER. I do not think we can be committed to a prudence which is pure inactivity. Prudence is an active and positive virtue. There are many factors one has to weigh—

personalities, one's own motivation, the good that emerges from doing something, the evils that may emerge if one takes action. But religious are not called upon to abrogate their basic human rights or their inherent dignity as persons. If the situation were such that this were common to and necessary in religious life, then the comparison sometimes made between a totalitarian state and the religious life would be all too apt. In unjust situations, the individual and the group must exert pressure, gently, quietly, *suaviter sed fortiter,* insistently but mildly, to improve the situation. The truth, too, has its own force and will emerge gradually, as history has proved. If it emerges *too* gradually, religious life will be extinct. Abuse of authority has caused much sufferings. The kind of careerism which denies principles to maintain positions of power is contrary to the notion of authentic witness to Jesus Christ. Everyone has to take a stand somewhere. It is for each individual to determine where that stand is to be taken. At times, it is not, however, a matter of free choice—but a question of basic moral law. We cannot destroy other people's personalities or deny basic rights in order to achieve our ends, howsoever "religious." There are certain absolutes we have to observe. Within that framework there are many prudential decisions to be made. If we abrogate the need for such decisions, we ought to close shop.

QUESTION. "I wonder whether the basic insights of the founder or foundress are obscured more by the institution or by the individual within the institution?"

ANSWER. There is an interaction between the individual and the group. Normally the founder's insights are not completely destroyed; they are repeated sufficiently often in their original formulation to stand as some kind of platonic ideals which recall to both the individual and the group the nature of the original insight. Are they damaged more by the individual or the group? Most religious groups are hierarchically organized and therefore power generally resides at the top. Hence, ideas are formulated more at the top—whether they should be or not is another question. Hence, Superiors are placed in a more favorable position to increase knowledge of the insight or to decrease it. But there is also a reaction of the group, and this reaction, particularly in this century, is becoming more palpable and more formidable. We do not yet have the polling of opinion that we should. If we had, we could have a certain pressure from the group which might weigh against the statement of an individual. Granted that both are willing to open themselves in a mutual availability of charity, we will evolve a dialogue. In dialogue, one might evolve mutual understanding, mutual concession, experimentation. But if the group as a whole remains passive to dictates from on high, then we cannot really blame those on high for dictating. They are not receiving the illumination or the resistance that would make them consult their conscience, tradition, the Institute, their founder's ideas, or the Holy Spirit.

QUESTION. "What are your views on a temporary vocation? How is it to be understood?"

ANSWER. Many theologians admit the vitality of this concept. It exists when there is a clear indication of the manifest will of God that this individual no longer has a vocation, for example, because of physical or mental ill-health. If, for example, a man's intellectual abilities are such that it is inconceivable that any work by this group could be enhanced by his contributions, we can say that there is an indication here that he would be better somewhere else. That doesn't really say much because the question does not usually arise in that fashion. The way it usually arises in the concrete is this: so far as all the objective criteria of a vocation go, the individual has them. However, he is no longer convinced that he or she *can exist as a human being* in this group. What shall we say to this? One can appeal to the mysticism of the cross, as is often done. One can err in two directions, it seems—by excessive supernaturalism or excessive naturalism. Some would say that it is the clear intention of God, having once given a man this vocation, that the man remain there even if he is destroyed in every way. I would rather have *God Himself* say that. Or can one err in the direction of naturalism? This is one of the difficulties, I think, with certain vocations today. They wait one year for the plentitude of their talents to develop in an absolutely ideal situation; then they may wait another year, and then, if it seems quite clear to them that the situation is not going to change for the better, they leave. We have to have a certain sense of the organic stages of time. We have to have a certain spiritual patience. For how long? That is a moral judgment. If a person says that, after prayer over a lengthy period of time, he is convinced that, given the concrete situation that exists here and now in this group, he does not belong there, I would not object to his leaving. But there *are* changes on the horizon, the far distant horizon; a little rosy cloud off in the dawn indicates that the situation may change for the better. I would hesitate to advise someone to leave religious life to which he has consecrated himself, and then find that the following year all his objections to this life have been solved. Temporary vocations exist. Who is to decide if this is one? The individual himself!

QUESTION. "Most of the community life is not carried on in a democratic fashion. Would seeking for more democratic dialogue be an attack upon religious life itself?"

ANSWER. No. There are certain details of organization of religious life which are very small, very petty, such as a command to walk up the left side of the stairs, and down the right side. It would be very immature to object to these details and to submit all of them to the community judgment. The community might not be interested in such petty routines. But in objectives which concern the work of the community and commit the community as a whole to an objective over a number of years, consultation is called for. I cannot see anything irreversible in the idea of a monarchical form of government. While the Church is *de facto* monarchical, certain democratic procedures could be introduced into the Church and into religious life. Most monarchies which exist today are fairly well limited, not only by their constitutions, but also by the will of their subjects. It's a rare monarch today, except Oriental potentates who are *not* the ideal norm for a religious Superior, who would impose on his subjects programs which are profoundly unpopular. Moreover, no matter how much discussion is engaged in, the decision is going to be made, according to the constitution, by the Superior. He should first hear the opinions of the subjects. It may make his decision more intelligent to hear all objections to it. The good ruler, even one who has absolute power, would want to know the state of affairs in the concrete, would permit and encourage democratic debate. On the basis of that debate, he would make decisions—sometimes, *very reluctantly*, contrary to common opinion. Usually his attitude will have been enlarged and modified by the open debate. The area of experience which subject religious have today is much broader than it was in the past. At one time, the abbot of the monastery may well have been the baker, and the butcher, and the cook, and swept the floors and done everything he commanded the subjects to do. He could rationally feel that he could give directions on how to accomplish these duties. Today, few Superiors have all the experience of their subjects. It would seem irrational, stupid, and unchristian to refuse to consult subjects in those areas where they are expert.

The individual is not simply a factor in the community. He is not simply a depersonalized item in the community; there is a reciprocal flow of good from the individual to the community and from the community to the individual. All have to contribute. And the group, the community, is made more vital by individual contributions to it.

QUESTION. "Do you approve of the existence of priests and religious in education and in the intellectual apostolate?"

ANSWER. Yes. They ought to have flexibility, mobility, and openness to do whatever they can do effectively for the Kingdom of God. Educational decisions should be made on the motives we proclaim—that is, supernatural motives. Whether we should continue in higher education today to the extent that we are now engaged is a very debatable topic. There are some who feel that we are in higher education for materialistic reasons. We have these institutions. They make money for us; they support us. If we are in a situation where Christian principles could not be expressed freely and in an open atmosphere unless we had our universities, then let us keep them. There are cogent reasons for Catholic universities in mission countries. I am not sure that most American cities can be considered a mission country. We have too many Catholic colleges and universities.

QUESTION. "Can we honestly state that our objectives are always quality? Do we spend money according to excellence?"

ANSWER. Some say we give a splendid formation, theologically and philosophically. And yet, perceptive souls say that the philosophy and theology departments are often the worst in a Catholic university. If so, is this an indication of that mixed motivation which we mentioned before? Let us have the willingness to discuss these matters. Let us realize that the laity is emerging and will continue to emerge, and will soon be prepared to take over certain functions once undertaken by religious. As for the State, certain evangelical principles have leavened it, and it has an ideal of justice. Very often it has taken over works once identified with the Church, charitable works and works of mercy. If the State can do this more efficiently, we should be willing to leave this to the State and to take up other works.

QUESTION. "What can the individual do who has certain insights, not shared by the group, or not shared by the Superiors?"

ANSWER. He can always form public opinion. Public opinion can seem like a very small matter. We would like to get rapid results, and casual, gentle, insistent contributions to public opinion can seem like a very small apostolate, but it is not. Theoretically there should not be this kind of blocking of channels:. The lowest member of a religious group should be able to go right to the top. There should be mutual availability and accessibility. Usually, however, there is not. What is the individual to do? Every individual will act differently in his situation and according to his competence. One man may give a theoretical contribution that will affect thousands all over the world, because this is his area of competence. Another area of competence may be different. We are all called upon, in whatever measure we can, to contribute to the formation, not of a spirit of rebellion, but of a spirit of open discussion. Of Pope John it was said, "Once one opens certain windows, it is difficult to close them again." Once certain ideas have gotten abroad, and certain reactions have been formed by mutual discussion, it will be difficult to shake convictions. The question of civil rights is a case in point. Once certain acts had occurred, it was no longer possible to return to old attitudes or to suggest that this was not a moral question. It is intensely annoying to an individual who sees what should be done and is limited by circumstances to a very minor rôle. That is also part of our historic vocation in the situation of the Church today. This is perhaps part of the built-in frustration that goes with a vocation in 1940 or 1950 instead of 1990. What can we do? Whatever seems prudent within the framework! Often this appears to be very little. At least we have tongues and pens and friends and influence. Perhaps we can win more friends and influence.

QUESTION. "What is the role of the religious Institute with regard to living out the charismatic ideas of Christianity itself?"

ANSWER. I would think the religious Institute would be a specified form of Christianity with certain means, specifically adapted to bring one more easily, *if* they are fulfilled in their inner spirit, to the core of the Christian spirit. It would be a function of the Church. We should find ourselves in unison with her heart because of the instruments we have at our disposal to understand her ambitions, desires, and her conscience more fully. If it came to this, that a religious institution, by pursuing personal aims, opposed the manifest will of the Church, it would act contrary to the insight of its founder. If a religious Institute, by pursuing a type of concrete, de-limited, ritualism, eluded the major issues of Christianity, it ought to go out of business. That could occur if the multitude of tiny obligations become so central that one forgot that there were central Christian commandments and insights, such as justice, truth, charity, equity. We would then be out of touch with the Church. Certain religious Institutes, for example, so de-limit silence and detachment that one cannot even visit one's dying father or mother. They should reformulate this so that it would be more in tune with the basic insights of Christianity on filial piety.

QUESTION. "Could we redefine the religious life canonically so that it would be less monastic and more apostolic?"

ANSWER. I do not think that canonical definitions are going to effect much. We have many definitions and descriptions, and the essence can remain vague. With regard to the question of moving a little farther from the monastic and more toward the apostolic, this could be arranged internally. I think that this is one of the prime causes of conflict in the religious life today. No one seems willing to specify exactly what we are supposed to be. Many Orders have rules that indicate that they are sixteenth-century monks, and works that indicate that they are twentieth-century laymen. No one seems willing, honestly, to face this conflict. If there is a rule which says one must inform the porter when he goes in and out during the day, one ought at least to have a porter! Some rules are obviously meant for a form of life that was monastic. We are to be separated from the world. That is wonderful and good; it is a beautiful vocation. But let us make up our minds so that we do not become schizophrenic. A hospital nurse doing active work all day long should not be subject to rules which would only befit one who has nothing to do but pray—an enviable vocation. This conflict is something we have to resolve. When the bell rings, leave the letter unfinished! God help you, if you leave the experiment or operation unfinished. Let us put these conflicts down in black and white, and discuss them. What causes anguish of soul is that no one seems willing to make these decisions. From top to bottom, they are left to the individual, and God help the individual if he makes them in a way unpleasing to those who should have made them and did not.

THREE · FREEDOM AND AUTHORITY: RECENT DEVELOPMENTS

THE TOPIC OF freedom and authority is particularly delicate. Unless, however, we believed in the reality of authority, we would not be examining it. We believe that Christ committed to His Church an authority to govern in the spiritual order and that this authority continues to the present day. It continues also in those microcosms of the Church, religious Orders. It continues to effect religious personally and individually. Believing fully in the existential reality of authority, its need and legitimacy, we re-examine the uses, the abuses of authority, and its nature. This topic is fraught with psychological traps. If we were to re-examine the notion of poverty, there would be no freezing into rigid positions on either side. To re-examine humility might cause boredom. But in any re-examination of freedom and authority, certain tensions immediately arise. Is this perhaps due to a kind of subconscious fear, on the part of some, that the structure itself might crumble if we submit it to drastic re-examination? Is it due to the conviction that in this virtue of obedience we touch the archetypal virtue of Christianity? That is, of course, false, for love has been and will be the central Christian virtue. At any rate, the topic engenders a certain emotional voltage. It must be discussed with the greatest discretion.

In any discussion of it, several objective norms should be aimed at. No writer will fulfill them all adequately, but at least we have them as norms. If we do engage in a loyal criticism (something that need not imply a dichotomy) of procedures of authority, we do so with the hope it will be constructive. Out of it should come principles and norms to aid the Church in her government, norms which will guarantee freedom, not from the existence or the enforcement of law, but that primordial freedom guaranteed to every human being as a human being, freedom from the arbitrary and the irrational. A critique of authority should not aim at a sterile list of defects, historical or present, in the Church. A loyal critique should manifest no *schadenfreude* or malicious joy. An enemy may show this when he finds certain blots and blemishes on a not-yet eschatological Church. The Christian rather hopes for a rational establishment of norms, guiding lines subject to reason, and, consequently, able to be subjected to the operation of the Spirit. The spirit has great difficulty operating upon an irrational content.

One would also hope that a loyal critique would proceed without rhetoric, not absolutizing personal positions. Such a critique is not an attempt to score points or to win a battle, but rather an analysis which seeks to establish with reverence, with discretion, with concern, submission, and quietude what is or is not the will of the Spirit and the will of the Church concerning this topic today. Such a critique obviously does not aim at endorsing present power structures, vested interests; nor can it be a critique which gains a neurotic security at the expense of objective values. It should be rather a critique which aims at moving within a climate of reverence, not only for the ideal Church, but also for the concrete historical Church in all the aspects and manifestations of its legitimate authority, even where one may not agree with certain emphases or certain aspects of authority. Christians must reverence, moreover, not only authority in the abstract, but also the persons who hold that authority. To these persons, even though they be in error, we still owe reverence. All men are limited; all insights are partial, defective. History may pass a judgment upon the most brilliant contemporary ideas different from that of our contemporaries. Any critique must discuss positions held by present authorities with great reverence for those authorities. It would be childish and naïve to expect to be governed exclusively by a combination of geniuses and saints. Christ, in conferring His mandate of authority upon the Church, did not guarantee that authority would be exercised exclusively by geniuses or even by theologians or experts or saints. The first rock of the Church was also the rock of scandal: Peter was not always particularly bold, open, or fearless. He was, rather, by temperament, a compromiser. Were one to choose between Peter and Paul on the basis of sheer intelligence, Paul would win. But authority was given to Peter. We may recall, however, that Peter listened to Paul; Paul withstood him openly to his face and Peter listened to him. Both Peter and Paul are saints. Intelligence, insight, historical perception, prophecy, genius—these are gifts of the Spirit. The fact that one in authority is stupid, untrained, oversimple does not mean that he does not govern with the authority of Christ—and often with the insight of Christ. He may have that insight which comes from existential contact with reality, which is not always the same as that of a theoretician.

Truth normally lies in a certain polarity or tension of relatively opposed positions. A Christian, in examining authority, should not wish to assert an unbalanced attitude, but to take into account the balance and the counterbalance of every truth. He should engage in a dialogue between opposing positions. The Divine Mind unifies within Itself a kind of *coincidencia oppositorum;* that is, in God, attitudes apparently opposed, and which would be opposed in us, because of our created limitations, are absolutely identical. So also a theological truth is able to incorporate vital insights from both sides, the conservative and the liberal.

Nor should one assume bad faith because another does not belong to our side of the discussion. We should be patient of criticism, for, if we are interested in making truth appear, it should seem normal that there may well be rational objections to our positions. These should not be discounted as attributable to malice or ill will. "Not that I may have the upper hand, but that the truth may appear," St. Ignatius said.

This awareness of the polarity of truth should not, of course, induce in us anything like an apathetic attitude, an attitude of spectator Christianity—"let the others fight it out; let George do it; I am on the sidelines; I am watching the game." No Christian can endorse that attitude and remain a practicing Christian. All Christians are "in the game," each according to his individual capacity, vocation, gifts, and limitations. All are involved. It is not a question of a first team, the ecclesiastical superiors, and we the second, third, or fourth, or the non-team, simply watching. In re-thinking freedom and authority, we have to be committed to prayer and activity, to the expression of public opinion, and to the formation of public opinion.

There are also certain undesirable subjective attitudes which militate against ever attaining anything like truth in this disputed area of freedom and authority. One of these is the desire to shock. Almost anyone who has any knowledge of history can present the most extraordinary, shocking statements if he marshalls them all together behind his proposition. He can turn most heads dizzy. This is simply playing the *enfant terrible* in the Church. It is not the Christian vocation to indulge in sensationalism—unless the truth itself is sensational. In that case, we should marshall our forces behind the truth and reject the sensational aspects.

We must also fear the scandal of the weak, the innocent. How "innocent" anyone is in the present modern world is not entirely certain, but one must be sure not to place stumbling blocks in the way of his coming to the truth. Neither can he who initiates a critique of authority yield to a fear of scandalizing the pharisee who is unwilling to see that we live in a Church still human, with all the glory and all the torn, divided quality, all the anguish of a Church still marked by sin. We must work in the shadow of the redemptive cross, the true mark of Christian humanism.

The mystery of the cross and the mystery of the resurrection loom large in Christianity, and obedience to authority will often demand suffering. No authentic theology of obedience can exclude that. Christ said it was necessary that He suffer and so enter into His glory. The crucifixion is not an event peripheral to any human problem considered in the Christian perspective. Obedience to authority may necessarily cause moments of suffering, moments when all are tempted to impatience. The Christian must then recall that the mystery of the crucifixion ended in the resurrection and that these mysteries cannot be divided in Christian thought or Christian meditation. We cannot omit consideration of the cross. It will always mark the Christian apostolate, and it will often mark obedience.

The second subjective attitude which will promote discussion on freedom and authority is confidence in the Church. This deep Christian hope in the Church is not based on trust

in human ingenuity or the evolution of ideas or the evolution
of history, but on the action of God breaking into history to
save us. The unexpected, the uncalled for, the free thrust of
the divine initiative into our history to save, to judge, and to
manifest His sacred intentions should animate all theological
considerations. Christians need to be content with the
rhythm in which God continues to bring out the truth. The
light may not dawn yesterday or today. We need a divine
impatience, and also a great patience. We need a respect for
the rhythm of time. We are not the sovereign lords of time,
even though we would naturally like to be. This respect for
time, for the *kairos,* creates in the adult Christian a kind of
patient urgency. By this I do not mean a kind of gradualism.
I do not mean that kind of attitude that states to the Negro,
"Bide your time for another twenty centuries and surely the
democratic processes of America will secure your rights."
No! What I mean is the kind of prudent employment of
every means here and now available and prudentially useful
to us, with the realization at the same time that the divine
intention for results and the divine schedule may be somewhat different from our own. Prudence does not mean a
program of inactivity, of doing nothing at all. Prudence is an
active virtue. It does what it can, wisely, to secure the de-
sired ends by the available moral means.

A fourth attitude useful in initiating this discussion is
freedom from resentment, from the bitterness which sometimes results from man's experience that the truth does not
convert men at once. At times it seems that there is a power
structure which proceeds with a pachyderm immobility
toward its ends, while all the processes of rationality avail
for naught. This bitterness, freely admitted, can envenom
even the truth. It can embitter the wellsprings out of which

leaps concern for that absolute value, truth. Along with freedom from resentment, the Christian can plunge himself constantly deeper into the genuine anguish that the Church-in-
crisis is experiencing. That is difficult because frequently
that which is prudent, which is discreet, which operates
sufficiently well at this moment, which preserves existing
structures, which supports institutional goals, is idolized as
though it were the absolute ideal. Men must have, in their
own limited, constructive way, an anguish for the truth
which is not easily come by. We must incorporate into our
subjective attitudes what Paul Tillich describes in his book,
The Courage to Be. The Christian must be an individual. He
must take, toward this debated position, toward this controversy about authority, a stand which is individual, which
represents his personal insights, represents a result of his
prayer life, of his action, of his listening to the Spirit, of his
experience of life. No Christian can be content to be simply
a cipher, a unit in a series of indeterminate objects. He must
have the courage to be and to be outspoken. With frankness,
outspoken witness, he must combine docility. If he does not,
he will not be able to operate effectively. The indocile, stub-
born, hard-headed, and resistant-to-authority cannot establish that atmosphere of peace which helps truth to emerge.

We are all aware that in the past great men have suffered
reprisals for speaking for the truth. Yet, it is God who is the
Lord of time, and temporary reversals are in God's Providence. We all know of the great charismatic prophetic voice
of de Chardin and how long it was silenced. Can we not ask:
If Father de Chardin had not chosen the obedient path he
chose, would his work today have the enormous influence
that it does? Who can describe the processes of the Lord?
His ways are not our ways. No matter how much we know

about Him, He remains the unknown God. Our knowledge is always a dark knowledge; our understanding of His ways will always be obscure. Neither philosophy nor theology, neither insight nor experience, has any completely adequate answer to the mystery of the cross. Christians do not impose the cross on anyone. They do not claim that it should be, in the normal social conditions that we provide, the constant vocation of the normal Christian or religious. But with frankness the Christian, and especially the religious, must combine docility and readiness to suffer. He must also be aware of the different ways the Spirit speaks to different vocations. Some are militant, thank God. They were born to be militant witnesses to the truth of Jesus Christ. Some are martyrs. The martyrs today are ordinarily the intellectuals, the scholars, who spend years evolving one theoretical point of one insight into one aspect of one problem. They, too, contribute in the same fashion. Nor should one be surprised if this problem of freedom produces not only difficulties, but occasionally even persecution. Has this not always been true? During the crises of the past, for example, did not the great, gentle St. Francis of Assisi suffer persecution? Did not St. Ignatius Loyola, a most prudent man—supernaturally prudent, not with the prudence of the flesh so common today —did he not suffer persecution, and not only from the world, but from officers of the Church? It should not astonish the Christian to find himself at times in conflict not only with the world but with some aspect of the Church's authority.

There is always a danger of falsifying perspectives by an either-or position. Either we are called to outspoken witness to value or we are called to submission and docility. The difficulty arises from the fact that we are called to both. In every organization, howsoever religious, evil can install it-self. Men are imperfect, and men are sinful. Moral defects can show themselves at the heart of the individual Christian, at the heart of an institution which does great good. It is decisively the duty of the Christian to combat evil, no mat-ter where it appears, in the Church as a whole, in the hierar-chy, in a religious group. This struggle between good and evil characterizes all human life, and we should not be surprised to find it in religious Orders or congregations. Loyal, loving battle for the truth is then called for, not comfortable sub-mission to error or evil. Obedience today demands even the witness of martyrdom to maintain the primal values of truth and charity. This is Christian obedience. Obedience that stands outside truth and charity is not the obedience of either a genuinely human person or a Christian, much less of a Roman Catholic. Throughout history this type of obedi-ence, dominated and formed by love of the truth and of charity, has at times criticized the Church. Saints have been called by the Spirit at times to criticize the Church. Perhaps the Christian would not be tempted to say today, "What a scandal! The Church has an ass as its head." No. Nor would we say some of the other things that Catherine of Siena said, much less some of the things the honey-tongued doctor, St. Bernard, said.

The fact remains that the Christian has to feel with the Church and to think with the Church. The Church today does not so much need men who praise her as men who are militant, and obedient, passionately obedient and passion-ately committed to the truth. Men are needed who are will-ing to accept misunderstandings to bring truth to the front. With these objective criteria for discussion in mind and these subjective attitudes in view, we can discuss more profitably certain aspects of the problem of freedom and authority.

The crisis of obedience and authority or freedom and authority arises today from theoretical considerations and also as a result of certain practical actions. There are, in this area, certain signs of the times available to anyone who can read, signs which should make a Christian pause and think. In enumerating these signs of the times, I do not necessarily endorse them. They exist. A widely publicized sign is the so-called "new breed" which demands honest, open discussion and maintains that it finds little honesty or openness. It demands honesty, sometimes at the price of revolt. Rebellion is not a normal means to good ends, but rebellion has been used in the past as a means to obtain authentic values. Signs exist that are disturbing to many Christians. Some, mistakenly, feel that they can exist in the integrity of truth only outside the Church. This is, of course, an error. It is the error which led to the Lutheran revolt. On the other hand, we should not ignore this sign: there was a Council called just a few years before the Lutheran revolt. That Council, instead of considering those much-needed reforms, voted to decide and decree that the soul is the form of the body. This is a splendid acquisition of truth. It was, perhaps, an acquisition which might not have been so sorely needed at that moment. A few years later half of Europe was lost to the Church. A Council too can fail. When change is called for, we must change.

Another sign of the times is the emphasis in Rome on collegiality. There must be some kind of sharing of authority and of power. Among the laity, with the conviction that all who are baptized share in the ruling power, the regal power of Christ, there is a feeling that the laity should assume responsibility in the Church—not simply the responsibility of kneeling, praying, paying, and obeying. Catholics see also a peculiar new atmosphere of open criticism which has arisen in the last twenty years. They note the extraordinary freedom with which some Catholics criticize the Church. One may well wonder if this criticism has not produced some good results. There have also been a tremendous number of speculative questions raised in the last decade on freedom and obedience. Freedom, obedience, and authority are by no means easy questions theologically. We should keep an open mind and pray and study them.

We see today such objections to Roman Catholicism as those issued by "*committed*" Catholics. There have been manifestations at the Council of certain democratic feelings. When the Council was opened, in the normal tradition, the bishops were instructed to maintain secrecy about the proceedings. It seemed evident after about a week that few took this instruction seriously. Some revolted against it: "With conditions as they are in the modern world, why should we be afraid of the truth being known!" We noted also what is sometimes called the November revolt, which occurred when the Holy Father announced that he would postpone further discussion on the question of freedom of conscience and religion until another session. This provoked not only dismay and astonishment on the floor of the Council, but also some rather strong opposition. It was not quite the kind of revolt which occurred in past Councils when ecclesiastics took up staves and knives against their opponents. We have now come to a certain degree of civilization.

One observes also within our own country a distressing situation when clergy take up and leave their diocese.

Whether this is done with or without good reason, is not within our competence to discuss. It certainly is a manifestation that something is not entirely well ordered. If individual clerics believe that in a particular diocese they cannot act as committed Christians, something is wrong. That is a serious situation, calling for exploration and dialogue, if not stronger measures.

There are signs that not only the laity and the clergy, but also many religious feel a certain sense of chafing under authority today.

I think the chief charges that are usually leveled against religious authority as it is exercised in religious Orders and Institutes number ten or eleven. Possibly each religious can add twelve more, but these are the more common charges.

The first criticism notes that religious obedience, as it is practiced today, dehumanizes man: the man who accepts and fulfills the type of religious obedience demanded in the concrete, existential religious situation of today will end up less a man, if a man at all. Some claim that religious obedience as it is lived, in the concrete, tends to produce a eunuchoid docility destructive of personality. It is said that obedience produces infantilism—a childlike, unquestioning submission which militates against the individual's growing into anything like that personal maturity which God wants for him. One of the reasons for this state of affairs, it is said, is the peculiar and unnecessary secrecy that is often found in religious organizations and in their operations. Such unnecessary secrecy often functions either as a cloak for malice or stupidity, or both, a type of secrecy never tolerated in civilized civil life, but only in totalitarian countries. At times, of course, secrecy is not only useful; it is necessary. But the extraordinary lengths to which it has been developed causes criticism today. If a book is condemned with no reason given, a modern man who grew to adulthood in a nontotalitarian existence will probably be distressed, and quite rightly so.

Religious obedience at times does produce a kind of collective-ego opposed to real personhood. What is meant by collective-ego? The formation, by brainwashing of the Communist type, of a situation where myths are created and repeated and repeated and repeated to influence the personality and distort judgment and viewpoint. By mobilizing subconscious forces, particularly neurotic forces, often sadistic or masochistic, one can produce a kind of collective thinking in which individual judgment and rationality count for little. The individual is either consoled by the great myth, that is "our group," or he is coerced, by fears and pressures, not to dissent from the great myth. This, were it true, would be destructive, unhealthy, and vicious. How true it is, the religious can examine from his own experience.

At times studies that aimed at an objective evaluation of the situation have been prevented from appearing.

Basically, all these difficulties come back to the fundamental question: can one lead a fully Christian life in this situation, in this group? Even more fundamentally, can one be genuinely human? The God-given basic dignity to be a man—can this be preserved in the politico-sociological structure that obtains in present-day religious life? A sixth criticism that is heard more and more frequently today is that authority has been desacralized. By desacralization is meant the assimilation of sacred power to secular power. Sacred authority has its own nature, its own constituents, its own spirit, its own controlling theme. Has this been assimilated, in the course of history, to a power structure more aptly suited to political society, to a secular power structure of a type we don't know anymore, Renaissance absolutism, offensive even to an atheist, or to Communism?

Others note that because of the present understanding of authority and its function, religious life creates an atmosphere favorable to politics, and by politics is not meant the art of the possible, but rather that kind of base politics which implies the lust for power, and the manipulation of men, ideas, situations to obtain and retain power, at whatsoever cost to me and the others.

An eighth criticism accuses religious authority of indulging in "frozen history." The Church, some say, which is both transcendent to and immanent in history, became incarnate successfully and evolved with the modern world up to a certain point. But within this special realm of authority, it became "fixated" by a sort of Freudian arrested development. Within the realm of authority it remained at the peak of Renaissance pomp, splendor, absolutism, and never evolved beyond that. The rest of human life, however, did. If this is true, one can readily understand the kind of schizophrenic mentality produced in a modern boy or girl who enters into the Church or a religious group. If his or her entire secular experience in the world of business, education, politics, the family, prepared him for discussions, openness, dialogue, and he or she found in religious authority a power structure characterized by absolutism such that all initiative descends from on high to "below," we can readily see that he or she may suffer a traumatic division of the personality. A split personality could, and sometimes does, eventually develop, to the point of genuine psychological confusion, if not psychological disaster. That kind of "frozen history" is what the male religious teases the female religious about: Mother

Foundress chose the peasant costume of Brittany for her habit because in this fashion her daughters would not be in any way distinguishable from the poor. Now, some centuries later, this beautiful, hierarchic, aristocratic costume is easily distinguishable from that of all other women. Thus an accident of history is frozen like a fly in amber—or so it appears to some critics of religious tradition and authority.

Others charge against the theoretical formulation of religious authority that the deepest Christian concept of authority has become obscured because those administering authority no longer have the conviction that they themselves should be obedient! The Superior is, of course, obliged to obey the constitutions of the Institute as well as the inferior. Sometimes, one notes, this idea creates astonishment in the minds of Superiors. At times, when these constitutions are recalled to those who are supposed to be administering and obeying them, there results a mild or less mild astonishment.

Tenthly: canon law establishes and gives rights to the laity, to priests, and to religious. These rights should be explained to those who possess them. Are they? Ever?

Some also are confused by what seems to be an arbitrary personal selection by Superiors of the elements of a constitution which they choose to emphasize. While rigidly·insisting upon those elements which make government easier for them, they suppress or de-emphasize those elements in a religious constitution which lay heavy burdens upon a Superior. The subject, it is insisted, must consult the Superior before taking important decisions or undertaking major projects. Many constitutions insist equally that the Superior consult the subject before taking decisions that affect the subject. At times it seems to some that authority picks the laws it will obey.

When theologians consider the evolution of authority within the Church, they first note that its primary norm indicates that it was *not* a non-sacred authority. When one looks back into the Old Testament, he finds that the notion of secular authority was generally *oppressive*. God was seen as the One who *liberated* His people from this yoke of authority. Yahweh's authority was *for personal freedom*. The primary characteristics of the God of the Old Testament is that He is a living, personal, true God who acts in history to liberate His people, to give them freedom. The great symbol of that liberation is the Exodus from Egypt, when the Israelites were freed from *arbitrary* demands. God acts freely within history to bestow freedom. Freedom, in this revealed context, is immediately given a supernatural dignity which it would otherwise not have had. In all the nations which surrounded Israel, the king was God; in Israel, it was just the other way around: God was king. Only gradually is Israel allowed to have a human king. When she does, it is a concession to her human weakness. If she had been entirely faithful to the Covenant, entirely motivated by the moral will of Yahweh, she would perhaps have submitted entirely to Him without need of an earthly king. When God does concede a king to Israel, the king is in a unique position in that he is always a *subject*, subject to God. The king, the ruler, the authority, is always an obeyer; he is also a listener. Authority obeys. The king is to be the one who sees to it that the moral will of Yahweh is carried out and that the people of Yahweh, the covenanted people, are freed from anything *arbitrary*. Authority acts to free the people. There is no *absolute* sovereign in the Old Testament save Yahweh. The sovereign is always a limited constitutional monarch, just as in civil monarchies today. Authority is hemmed in by law.

The Jewish people also had the right to criticize the king freely and openly. Not only did they have the right to criticize, but God founded for them an institution which would embody their criticism. He founded the institution of the prophets, whose function it is to interpret the events of history for the current situation and to criticize the defects of the priesthood and of authority. In the Old Testament, the Messiah who was to come is presented indeed as a king with authority. But what kind of king is he? He is meek and humble. He is "David reborn," that is to say, this king is a meek king, a meek and humble king. Authority is humble: without pomp or ceremony or ritual or jewels or force— supernatural, religious authority.

When the Christian studies the New Testament, he does not note any radical discontinuity between it and the Old Testament concept of authority. He finds a constant insistence on the part of Christ that we grant obedience to God rather than obedience to ritual or law, such as the Pharisees represented it. He also observes in Christ, as He exercises authority, the controlling attitudes of meekness, humility, and openness, not hardness or pride or lust for power. Authority in the New Testament is a function of love, the basic virtue of the New Testament. Christ, the Good Shepherd caring for His flock, is the perfect figure of authority. The community of the Church is a community radically different from other types of community, and the character of authority there is also different. It is an authority of service born of *agape*, of disinterested love or concern. The Church has certainly a structure, a juridical side, but she is also "organized love"; and authority, to be recognizable as Christian, must display this openness, this charity.

Freedom from human respect was also emphasized by

Christ, and the freedom of the children of God is emphasized often in the New Testament. The Pauline insistence
that love and the vital principle of love, the Spirit of charity,
the Holy Spirit, surpass in importance the clearly defined
and controlled demands of the law, is known to all Christians. Authority in the New Testament is totally relevant to
the structure of the community and to the Spirit of that
structure, who is Love Substantial. The community in
which the structure was embodied was essentially a community of love, not of law. It had an end that was different
from the end of the secular state, namely, the supernatural
salvation of man. Man achieves salvation by the freely given
love of God, whose divine initiative pours it forth in abun-
dance—*charis*. Given the supernatural end of the Church, it
should be clear that the means she uses to attain her end will
be closely related to it and to her primary concern—man's
assent in love to God's love outpoured. Christian authority is
an authority dominated by this central theme of the New
Testament. That should be obvious, but often it is obscured
in practice. The means cannot be identical with the means of
other organizations since the ends are different. Force, bru-
tality, deceit, lies, Tammany Hall techniques, do not advance
the Church.

Means such as sheer power, force, are not means adapted
to the end of the Christian community or a religious group.
The words used in the New Testament to represent
authority are not the words which any man would use for
coercive power. One of them is *diakonia*, which means service. The Holy Father signs himself the "Servant of the servants of God." We might try harder to make it externally
evident that Superiors are *servants* of religious communities.
There is also another word used in the New Testament for

authority, which means openness, or mutuality, or a mutual availability of presence. We are open to listen to the other, to learn from the other. It also means presence *for* the other, that is, we stand with them against opposition; we bear their burdens with them.

The authority portrayed in the New Testament is an authority based upon love, charity, genuine love. Otherwise it is not Christian authority. This style of community—the Christian—obeys in a different fashion from those who obey other forms of authority. In a good family, direct orders are the last resort of a good father or a good mother. There is, in a Christian family, an open atmosphere of love that pervades, illuminates the intelligence, and persuades the will of another. This type of command, in love, obviously achieves deeper results than mere external performance. Almost anyone is bright enough to do fully what he is commanded and fully to frustrate the wishes of the Superior at the same time. That game can be an engaging exercise, but it does not advance the work of the Church or the religious group. The examples posed by Jesus Christ for those who are to possess authority are suggestive and sometimes surprising. They should be meditated on long and *frequently.* Christ is the perfect figure of Christian authority, and He washes the feet of His disciples. His disciples are to be like Him. They are not to lord it over people, but to be like little children, servants of all. A servant is not recognized by his desire to impose his will on others, but by his disposability. The type of power which God vested in His Church is unique. It is not domination; it is not the imposition of will, coercion, force, brutal massive power that sees persons as objects. No. It is the power, the persuasive power, of love and service.

The Apostles' concept of authority, like that of Jesus

Christ, was to serve, not to be served. The relationship of the individuals who are in authority in the Church to their subjects will be quite different from what it is in any other group. It will be based on mutual openness. It will demand love first of all. It will demand clarification of the intellect and inspiration of the will instead of training, secrecy, mystification, institutionalization, standardization, socialization, conformism, punishment, imprisonment, human death. Such means of obtaining obedience, Plato noted a good number of years—and Plato was not a Christian—are insulting, degrading, and dehumanizing to a human being.

Christian authority will also admit the existence of that natural authority which results from sheer intelligence, knowledge, experience, or natural insight. This intelligence is valid; it is a genuine authority. If a subject happens to know sociology better than his Superior, then he has genuine authority *in this field* and should be consulted. The use of brute force, of reprisals, of financial force, and especially the use of neurotic pressures of fear—these may be effective in the secular sphere. In the sacred sphere, they are destructive of men and opposed to God. They inhibit the work of Christ's Church because His Church has a different structure, with different ends and different means. Christian authority should be a command within the realm of love, and Christian obedience should be an obedience in the realm of love. If Christians are to survive and obey, there must always be this personal dialogue between obedience and freedom, between subject and Superior. Otherwise, even if authority is exercised by Pope, Council, Cardinal, or bishop, it is not Christian. The supreme example is, of course, the good Shepherd who knows His flock with an intimate insight and loves it with an intimate, personal, individual love. He is the authentic pattern of authority. If His example is followed, many of the problems connected with freedom and obedience automatically disappear. If Christ's example is followed, these criticisms against religious authority would have little or no force. Perhaps at present these criticisms do have force. Perhaps we have obscured the full Christian notion of authority. Prayer, study, reflection are needed—but far more needed are humility, love, and the study of the Christ-event in the Gospels.

QUESTION. "Can you suggest some reading on the theology of obedience?"

ANSWER. I think the best commentary on it is Karl Rahner's article, "In What Sense Is the Will of the Superior God's Will?" This expression does not mean that God would have given the same command that the human Superior gave. We cannot make God responsible for the inadequacies, personal, moral, intellectual, or supernatural of all Superiors.

But if a command is neither sinful nor clearly irrational, nor destructive of the apostolate, one should obey. Were the action commanded sinful, one would be forbidden to obey, by natural law. If it is simply irrational, perhaps bringing rational arguments to bear may convince the Superior. It is not likely that one will encounter an entire chain of higher Superiors who urge the irrational. But it does happen. It is possible, since they tend to support one another. Ordinarily the voice of the Holy Spirit will break in somewhere in the chain. One is quite safe in obeying if the command is not sinful and the entire chain agrees with the Superior's command. The good Lord has undertaken to bring order out of confusion and stupidity and malice. He has not assured subjects that He will bring good if they disobey.

These are not easy problems to solve theologically or practically. There is no specific moral value in giving one's will over to another human being as such. So there are complex problems in defending the Christian possibility of religious obedience. One could be safe in saying that an order is the will of God if, having pushed an issue to the top, all suggest that one obey.

QUESTION. "Much emphasis is given today to respecting the spirit of the individual, and this is excellent. But in practice, what happens if the subject appeals to the Spirit against obedience?"

ANSWER. In good government, the Superior does not decide what his will is and then impose it on the reluctant or non-reluctant subjects. Where an individual finds himself in conflict with a clear command, which he thinks contrary to the will of God and Christian morality, he should use all normal means to seek clarification. The Spirit may call an individual or group to protest a command they think contrary to a great human or divine good. I also recognize the possibility of *disobedience on the part of Superiors* when they are clearly out of step with the *expressed* will of the Church in a given situation. This may happen because of a blindness due to defective training or intelligence or insight. Some cannot grasp that a moral issue is at stake when it is obviously at stake as, for example, in civil rights. In such a case, the subject who obeys the will of the Church would be obeying the will of God, despite the fact that a given Superior may have directed him explicitly or implicitly contrary

to the divine will. The kind of dialogue that we have discussed would obviate many of these difficulties. If both parties are willing to listen in mutual love to the Holy Spirit,
these distressing situations would not arise—at least they
would not arise with such frequency as they do now. If we
engage in prayerful dialogue, we will be able to hear the will
of God. If we refuse to do so and continue, on the one hand
hurling directives of authority, and on the other hand child-
ishly rebelling wherever possible, we will not find the will of
God easily. These situations should not arise. They would
not arise if both parties acted as Christians, with humility
and charity. There are certainly times when an individual
must witness for moral issues he clearly sees—even though
these issues are not clearly seen by his present Superior, be it
the Pope. It would be a peculiar situation if one were such
"a government man" that today, when the government is
democratic, he is completely a democrat, and tomorrow
when there is an autocratic Superior, he becomes autocratic.
A man cannot be fully constituted by another's opinion.
That happens, but it should not. It does not indicate proper
use of the God-given gift of freedom. It indicates a neurotic,
distorted, immoral counterfeit of obedience.

QUESTION. "One of the problems of major Superiors is their
concern with the idea of mandates given by the Church to
the community. This idea frees them from creative experimentation in community life and especially in opening up
new works."

ANSWER. I seriously wonder whether the major Superiors
of that religious group have explained to the Church officials
that the mandate lacks realism or the difficulties and problems it imposes. Do they passively accept it as easier?

One would also have to evaluate the authority with which the mandate was given. One should be happy to accept the slightest suggestion of the Holy See. But one could imagine a situation in which the Holy See suggests something, but only as a suggestion to be freely accepted or rejected by the community in question. Perhaps they want to provoke discussion. It is not the normal procedure of the Holy See to inhibit creative experiment. The Holy See has often suggested adaptation. Some religious have been rather slow in bringing these principles of adaptation into practice.

QUESTION. "How do you think young women should be formed for the religious and apostolic life today?"

ANSWER. Women could probably offer better suggestions. It cannot be repeated too often that, if there are problems, *objective* studies should be made. From the evaluation made by professional and competent men, psychologists, sociologists, clinical psychologists, vocational counselors, educational counselors, "Superiors," and a large group of "inferiors," one will get some kind of common ground. All must do everything in their power to see to it that religious remain *individuals,* and remain able to contribute in freedom by their individuality to the group life. How one does this constructively in the concrete is a serious problem.

QUESTION. "Is it possible to have a religious community of 300? Is it possible for any woman to know 300 nuns well enough to be in any genuine sense a Superior?"

ANSWER. No! Often after 5, 10, 15 years of religious life, there is not even a basic minimal knowledge of what the talents, needs, and personalities of the individual religious are in so large a group. They are not tested to find out what their aptitudes are. If a Superior is handling three or four hundred people or one or two thousand, let us be honest. He is not a religious Superior. He knows nothing about these people. He cannot possibly function as a religious Superior. Large houses must be divided.

QUESTION. "How can we analyze our problems?"

ANSWER. Make some objective studies, and study the objective studies that have been made.

QUESTION. "It has been many years since the Church has been able to say, 'Gold and silver, I have none.'"

Answer. Agreed.

QUESTION. "We would like to know what is being done about all the unnecessary pomp and circumstance among the richer members of the hierarchy?"

ANSWER. I hope that in time they will abandon their pectoral crosses and their rings and some of their insignia of rank.

QUESTION. "If nothing is done about a more equitable distribution of money to the poor, why not?"

ANSWER. South American bishops recently sold a number of their estates and gave the proceeds to the poor. Perhaps rich religious groups (if there are any) should follow their example.

QUESTION. "Is it not already an advance that a growing number of people in the Church can grasp the fact that Christian poverty can be manifested without ecclesiastical pomp and splendor? Is this not already an idea that has touched the intellectual and is permeating others?"

ANSWER. This is already an advance.

We observe a number of very strong human motivations here. There are very few people in the world, however virtuous they are, who are willing to relinquish power or money once they have it. They may administer it well. But there are very few who willingly relinquish it. Once one becomes rich, he may administer money very well; but it is a rare individual who feels called upon not to administer his wealth, but to give it away completely. In the Gospel, the rich young man went away sad. It is a hard thing to hand over *power* or pomp or money, which represents power.

We can all convince ourselves that the money is being used in the best possible way—that is, the way we have decided on. Some ecclesiastics who have amassed the most money have also proved themselves the best administrators of money.

QUESTION. "What does it mean when the Church approves an Institute?"

ANSWER. When the Church approves the constitution of an Order, it approves this way of life as a certain path to sanctity for the individual if the individual observes the constitutions not only according to the letter of the law, but also according to the spirit of the law. It also approves the works which are mentioned in the community's constitution.

QUESTION. "Does the Church provide any means by which individual religious may find adequate help and protection with regard to serious violations of personal integrity on the part of Superiors? For example, Sister Mary, intelligent, well-meaning, and faithful to her religious obligations, is in need of answers to some serious questions. She writes for help in this matter to a higher Superior. The local Superior finds out that Sister has written to this higher Superior. The local Superior calls the higher Superior to ascertain the meaning of Sister Mary's letter. The higher Superior informs her that she did receive such a letter and also gives information as to its contents."

ANSWER. That violation of secrecy is a violation of the natural law, but some religious feel that they are exempt from the natural law. They should be dismissed, whatever their position, at once, as lacking the most elementary qualifications for religious life.

QUESTION. "I have witnessed this lack of integrity on the part of Superiors. The end result always seems to be the same. There is no place to go to have problems settled. Please urge that the proper amount of personal integrity be maintained by any member of the Mystical Body of Christ."

ANSWER. Unfortunately, what Sister says, is, in my experience across several continents, not entirely uncommon. There should be very definite instructions and clarification given to religious Superiors, both men and women, as to the natural, moral, and canonical law. The local Superior mentioned above should be at least removed within minutes and given thirty days meditation to determine if she is a fit subject for religious life. Canon law provides for protection of secrecy, not only to protect the individual, but for the viability of the Order. There are institutes conducted by canon lawyers for Superiors to apprise them of the fact that they must obey the natural moral law and the expressed will of the Church in regards to these matters.

QUESTION. "If one's community seems to be closed to the medium of dialogue, how can an individual or group seek to alter this situation?"

ANSWER. This is a difficult question to answer. I think we have to face the fact that it is not just a rare malcontent who asks this question. There are communities which, perhaps because of the influence of one outstanding personality, tend to create a climate of opinion in which dialogue is rendered difficult. We have to admit that.

QUESTION. "What can one do?"
ANSWER. One can protest to the Vicar for Religious. It is, however, not unknown that Vicars for Religious, in defiance of moral law, have told the Superior not only that a community felt or said this, but that an individual in the community said it.

QUESTION. "The situation is such that the individual subject may not express her thoughts unless they agree completely with the administration; reprisals are too great. The end result is apathy, insecurity, fear, disgust, moral nausea."
ANSWER. With regret, I admit that in my experience this situation is not entirely uncommon.

QUESTION. "What can one do?"
ANSWER. Faith in Christ helps. Perhaps time will bring out the truth.

QUESTION. "In the meantime heads are being lopped off, talents destroyed, individual personalities crippled, and the work of Satan going on apace. What can one do?"
ANSWER. Again, we need a basic realism. All one can do is what seems possible in the situation. One cannot form a counterpower group within the community. Such a community shares in the crucifixion. Prayer, calm, and suffering, in

the hope that suffering will be orientated by God for the good of this community: this is all that is possible in some cases. In a realistic fashion, weighing the good against the evil, the possibility, the probability, the moral certitude of reprisal versus the moral good—gently, one can express an opinion.

QUESTION. "If the situation described represents what is common in religious life, clearly the religious life should cease to be."

ANSWER. If the situation described is common in one group, God wills that that group cease to be—absolutely and unconditionally—God wills it to cease to exist.

QUESTION. "Given two groups of people doing identical work, for example, teaching, or hospital work, one group composed of lay people, the other of religious. Does the authority of the religious Superior toward her Sisters differ from that of the lay Superior toward those working with her?"

ANSWER. The religious Superior has an officially recognized function within the Church, and she has committed to her the authority to direct and govern those under her.

QUESTION. "Is there an essential difference in the obedient response to religious Superior and the layman's obedience to a director?"

ANSWER. There is, on the part of the religious, a recognition of a clear and manifest will of the Church with regard to the Superior, *provided that* the religious Superior is commanding within the framework of her Institute, by the laws laid down by the Institute and approved by the Church, not by her whims and personal fantasies, likes, dislikes, moods, periods of the week, day, or month. If the Superior governs by the Institute, there is an objective difference because the Church has approved religious life as a way of sanctity and has examined it carefully before approving it.

QUESTION. "If there were no such difference, why take vows as a member of an active community?"

ANSWER. The vows have an objective value, as is traditionally admitted. They are equivalent to martyrdom. If one does not believe that, he need only try living them. Many religious today, such as the one described above, take vows which imply an apostolate marked by suffering. This is not intended by God. He would not have chosen it or approved of it. It is due to the stupidity or malice of an individual Superior. God did not want it to happen. But out of suffering can come good. Suffering within the Christian framework is not a meaningless frustration of human nature; it is orientated to something—collaboration with the redeeming Christ. This does not mean that I must do my best to provide suffering for others, needless to say.

⊡ FOUR · THE PERSON AND THE GROUP

IN PHILOSOPHY, psychology, and theology, the emphasis today is put on the person, underscoring his unique character and circumstances. In this chapter, I will discuss the person and the group.

This question is equally as controversial as the previous one—in fact, more so, for the question of freedom and authority is, in fact, only a subdivision of the broader question of the person and his relation to the group. We are often asked whether in certain Orders the symbol of the Order, the habit or the name, acted to inhibit the full development of individuality—a question which must be discussed seriously. We have also noted that one of the questions most often raised among young religious is the question of personal fulfillment, both natural and supernatural: will I, in this group, find both natural and supernatural fulfillment; will I be able to function as a developed personality in the natural, spiritual, intellectual, and human order? If not, the religious concludes, legitimately and correctly, he should not belong to the group.

Another aspect of personal fulfillment emphasized today is the question of the loneliness experienced in religious life. This may seem at first quite an extraordinary question to be brought up in relation to the religious life. Loneliness may be presumed to be obviated by the individual's entrance into religion. A religious family certainly should not be a lonely crowd. Often they are! This question can be posed in even broader terms: for example, what is the ideal and the real relation of a curate to his pastor? Is the curate a person in

85

relationship to his pastor and in relationship to his flock? It can be asked still more broadly: is the ordinary organization of the Church "personable" in regard to the hierarchy? What about the hierarchy in regard to the Holy See? What about the laity in regard to the hierarchy? Are they allowed to have individuality, personhood, fulfillment, activity, contribution, security?

One important point which needs clarification is the relationship of the external work of the individual to the external work of the group. Modern men and women do not wish to be totally absorbed in large, corporate, impersonal apostolates. Well may we ask a series of questions on personhood:

If the most useless members of a religious group are those whose training was exclusively by this group, should this give us pause?

Contemporary men and women are impressed by the need of certain values not always recognized by Superiors—as, for example, the need of adequately trained spiritual directors to adequately form religious. It is standard procedure in some groups that individuals are put to the task of spiritual formation because they can do no other task. That observation is not bitter: it is merely objective. If so, to what values are the group which fosters or tolerates this actually committed? Secularistic efficiency, money, external success?

Concomitantly, the tension between the group's endeavor and the individual's often results in unproductiveness and inefficiency in work and in personal development, in emotional and spiritual immaturity. If by the age of 50, religious are still drifting, something is drastically wrong somewhere, whether the fault be that of the individual or of the group.

Religious life in some groups systematically reduces individuality and produces functionaries, roles.

Does religious life manifest a distrust of individuality, of specialized talent? This question, for some groups, must be answered unequivocally: Yes.

One wonders whether a social group is normal if personal fulfillment must regularly be sacrificed and potentialities regularly left undeveloped in the interest of the immediate needs of the organization. If so, who is to evaluate whether these pressing and immediate needs are valid needs, in authentic continuity with the original charismatic insight of the founder and the original goals of the organization? The group itself? By what means?

One often wonders why religious groups do not make use of the means available to business concerns to determine efficiency. Do they fear objective reports? Who, within the religious family, is to establish a hierarchy of intermediate, proximate, and ultimate goals? Without such a hierarchy the dangers of an absolute policy of conformity is present. The results are obvious: ankylosis, disintegration, despair.

Initiative and docility must somehow be united for the health of a vocation and of a group, its continuity, its viability. Robots or alienated individualists striving for total independence do not constitute a family.

Many religious feel that the modern religious is overly individualist in his attitudes. No one is permitted to be so openly, but perhaps secretly, in a kind of conspiratorial silence of the peer group, is he? Many "marginal individuals" have only a formal tie of interest with their religious family. Should they continue in it, and if so, how?

When large groups of religious are disaffected toward corporate enterprises, this ordinarily means dissolution. This situation demands both a re-thinking of corporate objectives and adjustments on the part of individuals.

On the one hand, many religious do not appreciate the dangers of excessive individualism; on the other hand, Superiors often are not aware of the dangers created by decisions not shared in by the group.

In more blunt language, are those in charge of religious formation absolutely truthful about what is likely to happen to an individual in this group? Do they consistently lie to retain vocations? Do they "whitewash" the truth?

The increased preoccupation with the problems of efficiency, competence, self-fulfillment, and apostolic effectiveness calls for even greater stress on the supernatural nature of motivation and perspective among both Superiors and subjects. Superiors, too, must obey the Church, the Spirit, and the Institute; often they do not. Supernatural motivation is not an acceptance and implementing of a completely natural perspective which has the seal of having been handed down from "on high."

These and similar questions point to a problem in relating the group and the individual, the corporate apostolate and the person in his uniqueness. The more pressing problem, however, and the more immediate one, is the question of the rôle of the individual in the group and his fulfillment as a person. A recent book on the religious life stresses that the creativity in the individual's life is due largely to the interrelatedness between the individual and group, the support given to him. An atmosphere of encouragement, of expansiveness, is needed and should be given to facilitate creative endeavor. Yet religious complain that this is not had. Jokingly, religious will say: God deliver us from the "charity" of our group. At times they will openly state: the charity of our group would be called hatred by good Christians—or, at best, indifference, apathy, unconcern.

Is it common to find normal, adult, warm relatedness of one to the other in religious groups as we know them today? Is this normative in a parish, the hierarchy, the episcopal college, or the laity and the parish, or religious families? Is it possible for the individual to survive psychologically if he does not feel accepted by the group and especially by his peers? Several scientific experiments throw light on this problem. In another century an experiment was performed on a small group of infants. From the moment of their birth, the experimenter isolated them from the speech of others, from the most easily given form of communication. He instructed their nurses to remain completely silent during their contact with these infants. He wondered if they would ever produce human speech. He did not find the answer. All the infants died. The cause of their death remains speculative. Perhaps the will of God, perhaps a contagious disease, perhaps the wet nurses were not too healthy, or perhaps the failure of human communication simply meant that they could not survive as human beings. How much genuine, open communication exists in religious families? What is the effect of its absence? Psychological and religious death?

In another experiment, a psychiatrist studied infants in a foundling home. He provided for all their material needs, clothes, food, care, toys, competent nursing. Each nurse, however, had eight children to care for instead of one or two, as in a normal family. Thirty per cent of the infants died in the first year, of various causes. Many of those who survived, without personal care, developed a series of physical, intellectual, and emotional disorders which bore a direct relationship to their age at the time of their being placed in the foundling home. The longer they were in the home, and the longer they had been treated collectively, efficiently, but impersonally, the greater the degree of personality impoverishment and susceptibility to physical illness. That experiment might raise several questions.

Is it possible that certain forms of religious existence today, while providing for the medical and dental care of their subjects, fail to provide a basic minimum of warm interpersonal relationships so that thirty per cent either die or are equivalently dead as persons, while others develop physical, emotional, or intellectual disorders? Has this question any connection with charity, perfection, or basic Christian goals?

In another experiment, aged people were removed from their normal surroundings and placed in nursing homes. It was found that unless one left certain lights on to establish familiar contact with their area, the aged tended to become disoriented. The conclusion is clear: unless familiar objects are in view, the individual may develop fear, confusion, and emotional upset. All these experiments show man's need for and dependence upon others for mental well-being. We are continually in relationship with others. Our personal identity develops healthily as a result of interpersonal communication. The lack of such communication can cause serious illnesses. Because of the availability of intercommunication today, in the physical order, modern man is distressed about any group's inability to relate easily and warmly to others. Men seem to feel lonelier and more helpless as time goes on. In order that a man may develop as a human being, he has to communicate with others at the physical level, at the psychological level, and at the emotional, spiritual, corporate, social, and group level. Even as adults, men need this. They have antennae and receivers for communications, other than ears. We receive thousands of intimations of the spiritual climate which surrounds us, even though these are not spoken. We must therefore ask ourselves whether or not modern religious groups as a whole provide that climate of warm acceptance of oneself and of others which allows men and women to develop into normal personalities. If they do not, then it is the clear and unconditioned will of God that such forms of life be abandoned. It is not the intention of God to produce frustrated, hostile, emotionally upset people under the guise of a "spiritual perfection," which is unchristian, unethical, and inhuman.

Certain psychologists feel that there is no distinction between spiritual maturity and psychological maturity. Some believe that an emotionally deprived or infantile person cannot develop spiritual maturity because he lacks the freedom to create healthy reactions toward his emotional difficulties and toward God. Some, who have an over-authoritative father, will resent authority all their lives and can also develop unhealthy attitudes toward freedom and the Deity. In so doing, these might suffer more emotional conflict than the ordinary individual. It seems, however, to other psychiatrists that a man with emotional conflicts may grow in spiritual maturity, supernatural maturity, more than someone who has experienced no conflict. This is by no means an endorsement of the theory that our merit depends on the difficulty of our situation. We must make a distinction, however, between natural and spiritual maturity—a distinction sometimes not made. When we speak of fulfillment, we must also ask ourselves in what fulfillment consists, for one who has accepted the primary doctrine of our faith: the Lord was crucified and rose. Maturity cannot consist exclusively in natural fulfillment. Our humanism must include the mystique of the cross, the necessity of the cross, otherwise it is not a Christian humanism. Granted that, we must also realize that it is the intention of the Lord to bring to natural fulfillment and development those talents which He has brought to a particular religious group. In the New Testament, Christ consigns to hell the man who buried his talents. In this perspective, what is the destiny of Superiors whose unshared decisions ruin the talents of their subjects?

In achieving maturity, the individual must develop close relationships. He has to feel that he is accepted and loved. Without this acceptance, he cannot fully accept himself, his personal identity; he fluctuates. There will be unhealthy reactions. One unhealthy reaction is that of withdrawal, sometimes confused by religious with the spiritual value of "detachment." The human mind tends naturally to avoid repetition of experiences which have been unpleasant. If there have been hurts or rejection in early interpersonal relationships, a religious can evolve a sort of touch-me-not reaction by virtue of which he lives in an ivory tower of coolness, apathy, and emotional passivity. This can work effectively for a time, but eventually it wreaks destruction to the personality. These "neutral" personalities, however, are often set up as ideals in religious life, are they not?

Another reaction characteristic of the ill-related individual is that vigorous, assertive, hostile reaction which proclaims an unreal independence: the individual is against everyone and anyone. Some feel that, having achieved this, they have come to personal individuality. That is a neurotic norm for personal maturity. The feeling that one does not need anyone, that he is utterly adequate in doing everything by himself, that he cannot be touched or hurt by others, is not a Christian ideal of independence; it is pre-Christian, pagan.

A third characteristically sick reaction is neurotic dependence, a kind of pseudoaltruism: "If I do everything that the other could hope for and expect of me, if I show an endless and infinite charity—(an identification with the Deity!)—if I show an endless and infinite amount of compassion, never stand up for my rights, always assume that the other is right, always give in to the other, always be dependent upon him for my self-approbation, perhaps he will like me." This is called humility, docility. These three basic reactions are common outgrowths of the difficulties that exist in interpersonal relationships in all groups, and particularly in the religious family. Fortunately, whatever goes on in the conscious, there are also unconscious mechanisms which defend the normal man against acceptance of these pseudosolutions. Sometimes these mechanisms break forth uncensored in a manner unacceptable to social feelings. One of the ways in which they break forth in religious life is the feeling of aloneness, anxiety, insecurity, scruples, of being stripped of the security which comes from genuine, easy, warm relatedness to others. Anxiety can show itself in many forms: fatigue, headaches, hypochondria, asthma. There are some religious who are so anxious that they never make decisions; some who wash their hands all day long; some who are scrupulous. The anxiety of others shows itself in more diffuse forms: they are never completely relaxed in any situation with any idea, with any person, with any object, with any problem—with anything.

Another typical reaction is anger or resistance or smoldering resentment. The mobilizing of one's forces to cope with a dangerous situation is normal. At times, however, anger bursts forth in a perfectly fruitless fashion. These bursts of hostility pose a problem for the group which is attempting to bring its members into that style of life, or social situation in which they can have adequate growth and development. Religious must be on guard against hostility when the family group is accused of not providing those circumstances, attitudes, spiritual, and psychological situations in which the individual can come easily to maturity. That may mean that they have not come to maturity. Egotism being touched, one tends to lash out with a certain amount of hostility.

It must be recognized that there is a widespread concern today whether or not religious life provides the normal sociological and psychic conditions for maturity. It is very easy to point to certain exceptional heroes and say, "There is a perfect personality, one who has achieved maturity in our group." Sometimes the answer may be, "Yes, *despite* all the sociological conditions provided by your group." Surely this type of answer is not an adequate defense for the group or for the situation. We need strict scientific studies. Does every Order have a resident psychologist, a resident sociologist exclusively devoted to solving its problems? Does any?

Sometimes the answer is given as follows: "Had this individual only observed his or her religious rules and intuitions, followed the directions of the Holy Spirit, he or she would now be a totally, adequately developed mature individual." Possibly. He or she might also be in a worse situation, if by the direction of the Holy Spirit one means simply the observance of those group-norms which flourish in a particular religious group. The basic question is not whether this individual is responsible for his ineffectuality, his childishness, his absurdity, his hostility, his aggressions. The basic question is: Does the group as a whole offer the normal sociological conditions for development, and, if not, what can it do to promote them? A certain religious once mentioned to me that he was visited by three friends who were psychiatrists. They discussed the situation in that particular house. One of the psychiatrists inquired: "Do you realize you have provided in this house the absolutely optimum conditions for psychosis—not neurosis, but psychosis?" He referred to cultural isolation, depersonalized relations, tasks without commitment, lack of charity, legalism, conformism, fear, threats, brainwashing.

We see today in religious life an extraordinary number of people who need expert, technical psychiatric care to preserve health and vocation. The number of such individuals is large, a fifth of the community often. Such situations cry out that something is amiss. It may be partly an inter-reaction between the present culture group which is undergoing severe stress and strain before they can become a religious family. It may be that the modern secular family has not evolved to emotional maturity. We also observe the large older age group which feels that it is has been undone or betrayed spiritually by conditions offered in a particular religious group; we ought to reflect upon that and on the remark of the young religious: " I do not want to end like *that!*" referring to the older religious of the group. Our thinking, our reactions, our development, our growth, are sociologically conditioned. We cannot become individuals by hauling ourselves up by the bootstraps. Religious life has to offer man a concrete situation in which the possibility of growth is realistically, concretely present. Otherwise it will foster the type of individual who prides himself on individuality, but is one large mass of reactions to situations, a fully conditioned Pavlovian dog.

Young people ask today: "Why is there not that warmth and continuity of experience and ready exchange of ideas and experiences and sympathies, that mutual shoring up, that bearing one another's burdens, which we describe in terms of interpersonal relations?" Is there instilled in religious, in and through their training, a type of fear of interpersonal relations? If this is true, we would have built into religious life the fear of normalcy! This would assuredly not be the will of the Holy Spirit. But is it true? These questions are not easy to answer, and we are not going to answer them all in one year. If at least we could initiate some kind of a relatively open attitude toward them, an attitude which would encourage free discussion and at the same time some type of dramatic awareness of what the conditions of normalcy are, we might be well on the way to an answer. We would then attempt objective, detached, scientific studies to aid us. We would beg our competent friends to help us.

It is not my aim to give a complete description of psychological normalcy. That is impossible because men are generally in an evolving situation. Normalcy is an unstable complex rebuilt with the assault of each particular situation, difficulty, interpersonal relationship. There is no such criterion of normalcy which allows us to state that this individual is 100 per cent normal, that individual, abnormal. Normalcy is a continuum with a graying of distinction between grades. We recognize certain ends of the extreme, especially the more unfortunate ones. There do exist, however, certain concrete criteria, certain general indications of normalcy. In reflecting on these indications, we might ask whether the sociological conditions in religious forms of existence today are such as would tend to develop the basic reactions of normalcy or to destroy them. This question must be posed, not in the ideal order, but in the real, present, concrete order. If the answer is that religious life tends to destroy normalcy, it should cease to exist.

Every individual will have certain non-free conditions attached to his personal development. If one happens to have a Viennese grandmother, he is likely to have a tendency to react in the same fashion as she. If one happens to be all Irish, he is likely to have some of the characteristics of the Irish, no matter how much he reacts against them. Even his reaction against them would be provoked by the fact that he is Irish. A man comes into existence with many factors that he did not personally choose. He did not choose his parents, or his grandparents; nor did he choose his whole line all the way back to Adam and Eve. Nonetheless, all of these individuals have contributed to the making of him. He bears the sin of the world. He did not choose the period in history in which he would be born. Yet, the period in history in which he was born tells a great deal about his personality, the form and shape of his approach to problems, ideas, situations, to groups, to the intellectual area, to the area of achievement, to the apostolate—to everything. Possibly if he had been born in the Renaissance, he would have fitted in much more aptly—Superiors who act like Renaissance princes prove this. But he was not, and he had nothing whatever to say about it.

Moreover, he did not choose his infancy formation: he did not determine whether or not his mother had another child at once, or no more for ten years, or whether she could give her undivided attention to him, or whether he had to be cared for by a nurse. Those factors, and the relationship between his mother and father—so much that was done in relation to him—the individual did not choose. If he had done so, he might have modified it in one direction or another. He did not choose his economic situation in life, to be born rich or poor, yet this influenced his viewpoint in many ways. Even theological problems are influenced by these considerations! We have therefore to note that many elements of our personalities will be, to a certain extent, influenced by non-free factors—*influenced*, not *determined*. Somewhere in his growth, man must realize that there are certain types of changes which are possible and other types of changes which are not possible for him. If I were born to be about six feet tall, I cannot become short today, even though that might make me less conspicuous and a less threatening figure to those shorter than I. If I were born stupid, there is not a great deal I can do about it; if I were born bright, there is not a great deal I can do about that. I can learn to curb my tongue and not to show my intelligence at periods of stress and in situations when it is neither tactful nor judicious. I can show a certain passivity and Buddha-like character which will conceal my genuine convictions, ideas, from others. But I always have to do that on a certain non-free basis. There are only a certain number of items open to any man's personality development. The more mature he becomes, the greater his say in what avenues he will choose. As a man grows toward maturity, he develops self-control—not control from without, from punishment or threats or neurotic fears or organizational patterns or ritual or indoctrination—but self-control, from within, his personal, autonomous freedom. He chooses certain goals, modifications of established goals that society allows, for himself. Whether he will be a writer, a teacher, a non-teacher, a non-writer, he determines of his own choice as he grows. In a mature man, there is a greater capacity for personal decision and a greater appreciation of and use of personal freedom. As one grows to be a person, he is influenced less by shoves or pushes or pulls, physical or psychological, and more by his personal interiority. The frequent complaint that religious do not seem to be able to make up their minds is an indication that such religious are still at a *pre*-adolescent stage. They have not so matured that they can determine their relationship to themselves or to others and to their environment, within pre-given limits and with certain self-chosen ethical goals characteristic of their ideals.

Ethical goals are characteristic of the mature individual, as well as a relatedness of these goals to the goals of society and of the religious group as a whole. If one is in opposition to the norms of the social group as a whole, there are certain built-in penalties, whether one is right or wrong. A religious in opposition to the group goals of his Order would be better off out of the group. There will inevitably be friction if I am a committed Christian in a Mafia-group. As an individual grows, he learns to stratify and modify his reactions in regard to himself and to others and to goals, and to see how they may be realistically incorporated into his concrete universe. He learns to judge with a certain flexibility, is able to see things, not in terms of extremes but in terms of nuances, shadows, distinctions. The people we live with are normally not angels or devils. Some approximate the one very closely; some approximate the other. The majority are somewhere in-between. In all, one finds a constant blending of attributes: some are very charitable toward themselves; they are not so charitable toward others. They are charitable toward this group of men, let us say, but not so charitable toward women. Some are especially charitable toward children, but not charitable toward old people. A blending of attitudes occurs in most men. Mature individuals learn to recognize that things generally exist in this kind of mixed state. Doing so, they learn to gain an insight into themselves. Even in oneself, things are normally going to exist in a non-totalized state. A mature person must have, then, an ability to tolerate himself and others. Learning to tolerate himself with a certain broad humor and understanding, the grown man learns to extend that tolerance to others. Of course, if he cannot tolerate himself, he will not be able to tolerate others either. Self-acceptance is a very important element in growth, and a religious formation which instills contempt for self is unchristian.

The mature individual learns to work matters out, not in stereotyped patterns of conformity to pre-existent religious, intellectual, or group patterns, but to stand at a distance and re-examine problems. His habitual ways of thinking can be altered in new situations. As a man grows in maturity, his sense reality increases, his non-denial of reality increases. All the willing in the world is not going to make black white, and therefore it is childish to dictate to being that it should be thus or so. This is the way it is, and therefore one must use realistic means to cope with it as it is. We must stubbornly face reality. If, for example, a religious Superior is stupid or vicious, an adult subject does not stubbornly adhere to the idea that God provided only intelligent, virtuous Superiors. He notes that he did not get as bright and as good a Superior this time as he did last time. Possibly with our help, the help of the community, the aid of the Spirit, the present one will develop. Maybe it will be refreshing to have someone who is not too bright or a little wicked. To deny reality is not to improve the situation. The mature person eventually realizes he has only a limited capacity to modify reality. Consequently, it would be better to use whatever energy he has to modify reality within those limits in which reality can be modified.

One often meets a type of immature religious who is dismayed that Superiors are not paragons of virtue. Whoever said they would be? They are made of the same common cloth that others are, and we are not all geniuses or saints. Nor is it likely that they will be geniuses and saints. If they were, they would be doing some other work, normally. However, in ideal cases, they possess prudence, balance, common sense, good judgment, safety. They do not rock the boat—too much in this direction or in that direction—and all get to shore more or less safely, as a result.

The mature person realizes his limited ability to modify a situation, and he works within those limits. He realizes also that this does not involve any complacency with the situation. Possibly the situation may call for absolutely critical measures. In that case, such measures should be taken, but only within the limits of one's power. The grown religious does not oversimplify problems or their solution. He respects the complexity of men, events, situations. Men and events are open to various interpretations.

A religious cannot achieve adjustment to reality and a realism in charity to others, unless he realistically appraises himself. Realistically to appraise and love ourselves is not quite so easy as it may at first seem. By virtue of original sin we all carry within ourselves a kind of hatred for ourselves, strange as that may seem. We have to learn to show a kind of divine benevolence toward ourselves before we can show it toward others. A divine tolerance, patience with ourselves, will show us that while we are not so bright as John, we are better looking; we are not so good looking as Peter, but we are younger; we are not so young as Allan, but we have more experience. This measured, humorous, balanced view is a Christian one. One who basically accepts himself, accepts the divine plan making him "this." It is not an easy thing to accept one's limitations and even moral faults without a pervasive, free-floating neurotic guilt, unattached to any object or disproportionate to the object, bringing dismay or surprise that one is a sinner. The Church is the home of sinners, and the Church has sinners within it. Religious must both love and know themselves. Knowing oneself takes a certain amount of depth—examination of conscience beyond that peripheral "dusting" which most religious engage in. It demands a kind of profound search for the real motive, the deep springs of action from which all our faults flow. It is not easy to discover the heart of the onion. It lies deep down. To peel off one skin of motivation after another is healthy. One starts with the first skin of motivation which is always very virtuous: "In order that God's glory may be greater, His praise may be greater." Underneath that: "That I may have a greater satisfaction"; then: "That I may get revenge on that person." And so one gets down further. At the heart we find something not always admirable. We will usually find that all our virtues and vices emerge from a common wellspring. Then we see the ultimate root spreading out in all these flowers of vices or flowers of virtue. Then we are getting a faint idea about ourselves. Having gotten to it, we should not suffer a moral nausea but rather make an affirmation that so it should be, utter an *amen* to this person, and try to improve. That kind of insight leads to growth.

The sane religious has a profound and ineradicable need for warm emotional ties with others, human, emotional ties; by this is not meant sentimentality, which is directed back upon oneself, but normal, warm, human relatedness, love of and affirmation of others. Because we are men, the rights of any segment of humanity are not a matter of complete indifference to mature men. We cannot block out what is happening in Vietnam or what is happening in the South. We feel a relatedness, a belonging to this entire group. A mature man will seek out, and need for his growth, involvement with others. One must be able to give and receive human affection freely, without fear of interpersonal relationships. Living as an isolated molecule, a religious will end up schizoid, unproductive, unhappy, unspiritual, unchristian.

Without fear for his own individuality, a mature religious learns to adapt to the group, to various types of human relationships so that he can have friends at various levels of commitment. All these relationships enable him to react more and more to a wider variety of human situations with affection and warmth. With a certain amount of ease in accepting others as they are in their uniqueness, he learns to understand himself more fully and to accept himself as he is in his uniqueness with the same tolerance that he directs toward others. This warm, stable, related type of individual will have certain profound, ethical convictions and ideals, and the moral courage to pursue them. His anger will not be provoked by routine details, but on important issues it will show itself strongly. A mature religious should incorporate his experiences into a dynamic pattern which makes him at ease with those who differ from him in ideas, ideals, experiences, age. In old age he should manifest a serenity and empathy, an openness and an ability to empathize with all age groups underneath and to encourage them, to be "with" them. Such a religious has come to serenity.

The mature religious pleases himself as well as others, accepts himself realistically, and is moderately content with himself—what St. Bernard meant by genuine humility. This is not to be content with oneself as needing no further development, but as accepting oneself with one's limitations, defects, disabilities while remaining moderately content with this concrete individual who has made some small progress toward sanctity and, with God's grace and favor, will make more.

Moreover, a mature religious has a realistic appreciation of himself, is able to evaluate the worth of a particular act or a particular motivation, a particular situation, a particular talent. The temptation of the extreme is a temptation to replace the Deity with oneself. If one can only contribute a count of three, one contributes three. Why not? It is more than two, which is worth more than one. All three are worth more than nothing.

A certain expansive attitude frees the mature man from the compulsion to be always at work, always in tension toward something. A kind of mania for work—characteristic of the American scene—may become a characteristic of our religious scene. We rarely seem to be able to sit back and relax and enjoy, to develop those natural contemplative organs which are to be used in the eternal kingdom, heaven. One's ability to enjoy beauty, leisure, companionship, the good things of life is a sign of religious maturity.

Religious should be able to enjoy the love, praise, and encouragement they receive without feeling embarrassed. If one can't accept love or praise from anyone else, then one can't give any praise or love either, not healthily, easily, humanly.

The ability to work with others, to accept direction, is a sign of maturity. Orders, of course, should not be given in a manner that indicates pushes and pulls, but with a kind of intimate collaboration with the person who is before one, as God gives His commands. His commands are always in a most intimate conspiration with our own better aspirations and values. A mature religious can accept orders calmly, if they are normal orders.

The adult religious knows when and when not to feel guilty. Why, then, does guilt seem to play so large a rôle in those who presumably are fairly good Christians? Religious should be noted for the freedom, independence, and joy of the children of God.

Mature religious are willing to try new paths even at the risk of failure. Is this characteristic of religious groups as a whole today? Are they terrified at any suggestion that all is not well with them, with the group, the school, the house, the Church, the Council? Can they admit realistically the possibility of error? Or of a failure? Or of the death of our Institute?

Mature, independent behavior implies the ability to live courageously and calmly without feeling threatened. It is curious how often one hears expressions which indicate that members of a religious group feel threatened by any change in position, change in authority, change in teachers, change in policy. Sometimes any change seems to undermine all the pillars of security underneath. Grown-up religious should adjust to such changes without feeling threatened; but do they?

A mature religious should attempt a realistic evaluation of

the shortcomings of his religious family and of himself, and this while retaining faith in both. One accepts one's religious family and one's companions with all their shortcomings, and neither rebels against them, condemns them, or denies the existence of the shortcomings. Charity suggests to us to love them as the Lord loves them with all their objective defects—even sins.

An even disposition, calmness, plus the ability to express anger when necessary, to fight for one's rights, is a sign of the mature religious; but a constant anger bubbling under the surface is not. Let us save up anger, as the Lord did, for situations which call for it. Instead of a thousand little pots boiling over, let us provide one volcanic eruption for an important principle.

Since a feeling of being accepted, or belonging, is needed for maturity, we reiterate the responsibility of the group to make the individual feel that he or she "belongs." If the religious is never asked his opinion about anything, then, no matter how calm and gentle, sweet, paternal, maternal one is toward him, he will never feel accepted as an adult. He may be accepted as a child, but he will not mature until he is accepted as an adult.

Being at ease with himself, a mature religious can accept dislike and misunderstanding. There are bound to be certain opacities in matter and certain channels of communication and understanding which are difficult to open between one man and another. It is a characteristic of matter to be impenetrable; therefore, we cannot know any individual completely, or like all equally, or be liked by them; and we must simply accept that.

The inability to make decisions without undue delay is

one of the characteristics which reveals most openly the immaturity of many religious today. Many cannot make prompt decisions except within the inner, personal, spiritual domain, in their relationship to the living God. They can decide to become more holy, to pray more ardently. When decisions involve external action, and are subject to objective criteria, to judgment, to criticism, some religious are too hesitant. Some simply cannot decide; these are fully neurotic.

Relationships of neurotic dependence, in which one's security demands the approval of another—so often seen in convents—should be discouraged. We should be able to stand outside ourselves and give to others independently of what we receive from them, although we hope for reciprocity of charity, as God Himself does.

Being a Christian, the religious must replace hate with love, so that he can approach a situation in which hate plays a role with tranquility, clarity, and patience.

Some situations, he will decide, he simply has to tolerate. I freely choose to accept a situation which objectively should never exist. This attitude doesn't destroy a religious. A grown man does not feel totally threatened by factors which make him objectively insecure. His value-system, his convictions are interior to him, "self-chosen"; and he defends them calmly, but stubbornly.

If religious groups wish to create a social atmosphere in which maturity can flourish, the first condition is a climate of warm acceptance of the other as other, not a theoretical acceptance, but an acceptance in the order of experience, an acceptance communicated and felt. Without this, religious life is doomed; and should be.

QUESTION. "I have for years watched young Sisters. I see them come into the convent with generosity and vigor. Before many years, all are in the same pattern. Must one ask them to sacrifice their initiative, their ideals, their personality to follow Christ?"

ANSWER. I presume the only reason Christ called them to religious life was that they had ideas, initiative, personality; unless, of course, He chose nonentities to frustrate His work. It is the function of the Superior to see to it that their ideas, insofar as these are accurate, that their personality, insofar as it is a God-given talent, that their initiative, normal and human, should be employed for the full development of the group. Occasionally, there will be an inevitable conflict between a corporate work and the realization of the ideas of an individual. If the Lord invited this individual into this group, presumably He knew this individual, including her history. He called an individual who would contribute to this group. If the Superior is unable to bring that out and treats the individual as a neutral quantity, he or she is going directly contrary to the divine will. Only a free individual can obey fully. If nuns are not free, they are not obedient; they *cannot* be, either with human obedience or sacred obedience. They can have the obedience of sheep, but the mere fact that a Superior is a shepherd does not mean that he is leading sheep. The fact that a Superior has a group doesn't mean that he should reduce the group to something like a herd of cows, which, as a group, can produce so much milk.

It is the precise individuality of the subject that is given to the group. There must be sacrifices on both sides. The individual personality *must* retain its creativity, otherwise the call to religious life *could not be a divine vocation.* A vocation to constant frustration of one's human attributes and ability is not in any sense a divine vocation. It is not even a human vocation. I would not recommend for any human being a marriage in which I saw that this would happen to his personality. I would not recommend a vocational career in which I saw that one would lose his initiative, ideas, personality. Nor do I think for an instant that it was the intention of God that religious should lose them. If one is to obey, to work for the group, he must obey in love, as an adult. God intends us to be adults. There must be more mutuality and more honesty. There must be more openness and a certain democratization in religious life. There should also be written, explicit guarantees of freedom in any organization, whether it is the Church itself or the religious family or the university or the school. There should be explicit, legal guarantees of future progress and of openness, of discussion, and of mutuality. The individual is supposed to be fostered by authority, not destroyed. He is supposed to grow, not become a mutilated, truncated, blinded, mole-like, unindividualized, neutralized mass of indifferentiated gelatin. Freedom of discussion should be encouraged. Instead of fear, institutionalization, thought-control, brainwashing, the personality should be tested objectively and its gifts developed, not truncated. If a group continues to suppress individuality, it is destined for extinction. It cannot but die, and from the divine point of view it must. The modern world is quite different from the world of the seventeenth century. For example: the position of women in the seventeenth century could result in a life for a nun that was not too different from that in the family. Woman today has achieved a position in secular existence and cannot be expected to abandon the attitudes of initiative and independence she gained in that world when she enters the convent.

"When Christ said to His apostles 'Come follow Me,' He did not lead them into seclusion. He led them to cities and towns. He mingled with the multitude and made many disciples. What about us?"

Many religious are asking this question today. The evolution of many religious Orders led them to educate their members in seclusion for fifteen or twenty years. This is just one more aspect of the problem we seem constantly to face: which are we supposed to be—monastic or apostolic or both? If we are supposed to be both, we must make adaptations. If exclusively monastic, seclusion is excellent. But an Order ought not be plunged into the monotony of the monastic observance if it is supposed to lead an apostolic existence. This destroys a vocation.

QUESTION. "Have religious in the U.S.A., to a certain extent, yielded to the natural tendency to install themselves in an apostolate which has proved successful, at least materialistically, and which involves moderate comfort and established routine? Have they shown the flexibility, mobility, to develop new apostolates?"

ANSWER. It seems clear that many are so installed. In some groups, alas, mobility is minimal.

QUESTION. "As an active community, we have been called to a social service vocation. Superiors, however, seem more interested in silence, recollection, places we are not to talk, visit our neighbor. And many of the spiritual books written to guide us seem more suitable for the guidance of religious of a more monastic trend. They place great emphasis on silence, recollection, prayer."

ANSWER. Basically, the Superior is trying to suggest: maintain a life of prayer. If she is unable to conceive of such a phenomenon as contemplation in action, she should study the topic. There are forms of prayer specifically adapted to active groups which can lead an active religious to a high form of prayer.

QUESTION. "Do you think it would be possible for a group of Sisters within a community to get permission to try a new way of life—such as working among the people for a salary and thus becoming a leaven among the people? Some of us thought we were going to do so in the first place, but find ourselves imprisoned behind convent barriers."

ANSWER. Religious ought to think seriously about methods of becoming more accessible to the modern world. They ought to modify certain antique usages, relics of a beautiful and gracious way of life which fitted a past period of history, but which do not fit our own. They must be open, accessible to the secular world—even Carmel.

QUESTION. "There are certain religious groups who work for a salary, aren't there?"

ANSWER. Yes. Such a vocation to penetrate the secular world is excellent in principle and very effective when carried out consistently. More and more such experiments will be tried in the future.

QUESTION. "Are the rules a means to an end or are they the end in themselves?"

ANSWER. I think that question answers itself. The end is

union with God, which consists primarily in affective charity —inner love for God and man. Charity is not two virtues, but one with a double object—God and man. The rules are means, hence, relative to that end.

QUESTION. "I had always thought that living a true Christian life was the purpose of my life in the convent. Now I am beginning to wonder. I am gradually straitened and harassed, cribbed and confined by a multitude of minutiae without Christian significance."

ANSWER. I think a certain modification of this routine should take place. The individuals in the group, after ten, twenty, thirty, or forty years, should have come to a relative maturity and be allowed to expand the area of their liberty and their individual judgment. By the time they are adult religious, they should have absorbed the spirit of the foundress sufficiently to exercise liberty, within the perspective of the original *insight* of the foundress. If a nun has not, after many years, absorbed these insights, it would be better to tell her, "Go out and grow up; and after you have grown up, come back and we will see if you are a suitable subject for this group."

QUESTION. "Please explain the obligations which Superiors have in regard to their subjects."

ANSWER. These obligations are spelled out in canon law and in the particular constitution. But the whole spirit in religious life is not so much one of obligation to subjects as to the Institute.

QUESTION. "What kind of person should they be and in what spirit should they act?"

ANSWER. They are to act within the mutual availability, accessibility, of a dialogue of love. The Superior commands; the subject obeys in the mutual exchange of love. Otherwise we have no religious obedience.

QUESTION. "If God calls a soul to serve Him in communal life and the soul responds, is there not some responsibility on the Superior to see that it is possible for this person to function in the Church in the way God called her?"

ANSWER. Obviously, yes. God did not just call any indeterminate group to the Order—He called ten or fifteen individuals. He did this because he wanted to use that individuality which He will never repeat for all eternity. Each is irreplaceable. Hence religious life must make it possible for each to develop to the full his or her personality. That is the clear will of God, and it is also the manifest will of the Institute and the Church. It is also the will of the foundress and of all who understand her. It is also necessary for the proper functioning of the group, even for a natural group.

QUESTION. "Cannot someone explain to Superiors that we are not all made the same? That we do not all function the same? That we are not all hungry at the same time?"

ANSWER. If there is insufficient respect on the part of Superiors for the concrete, God-given individuality of a person, we will not see happiness or productivity in religious life. Without some freedom of action, one cannot have the full deployment of the human and divine resources God has given to a person. If the Superior crushes individuality, he is not fulfilling his rôle as an administrator in the natural order or as a "superior," a servant in the supernatural order. The Holy Spirit is not given only to Superiors or to the hierarchy.

If He were, then they could be the only ones who belonged to the Church. The rest would be outside the Church. The Holy Spirit is given to all of us, and there is no reason to believe that the prophetic function ceased with the Old Testament. It exists in the New Testament. The Spirit speaks through each receptive individual, whatever his function, and all must obey Him, all must listen.

QUESTION. "Sometimes Superiors seem to wind us up like toys and we keep going until we are unwound."

ANSWER. That is a very important criticism. It is difficult to be responsive to all the nuances of the personalities with whom we deal, and yet we cannot play down the task of Superiors to foster freedom. The Superior is at the same time a listener to the individual and a listener to the voice of the Spirit. He is not there to shove people around as if they were objects, plugs in a switchboard, although in the past, many Superiors thought so.

QUESTION. "One celebrated theologian has said that the vows of religious liberate us for a service to the world otherwise not possible. This seems false in the real world. If it is true, why are we seemingly so unfree?"

ANSWER. Perhaps because the vows are not observed in the spirit in which they were intended. Perhaps religious are not permitted to so observe them. The vow of obedience, for example, calls a religious to contribute positively to the group to which he belongs. Perhaps experience indicates too often that contribution is not wanted, and, if given, reprisals will follow. If so, the religious is not being permitted to observe religious obedience. Concrete situations do not permit him to observe his vows.

QUESTION. How can we change the situation?"

ANSWER. Get a new theory, i.e., return to the original theology of the founder. Pacific means can be used, and a rethinking of one's traditions.

QUESTION. "Why are we seemingly unfree?"

ANSWER. The purpose of the vows, as the theologian quoted remarked, is to liberate us. They are supposed to be a freedom from impediments to union with Christ and Christ's beloved—the human world. Perhaps we need a new, or a return to an older understanding of them. Perhaps we need to see them more from the viewpoint of fulfillment and less from the viewpoint of mortification, more from Easter than from 'Calvary.

QUESTION. "Can you visualize the amount of good 180,000 Sisters could do if allowed to use their initiative and creative ability?"

ANSWER. It is a magnificent, stirring—even thrilling—prospect for the Church! I hope that despite many restrictive measures they can use them now. Restrictive measures may also be lessened further as the individual demonstrates more maturity. A wider area of creativity will then be opened up. That is normal. It happens in any family. When a child is three, he is told to sit there, to come here. When six, it is a little different. He has learned some things in some fundamental areas and is consequently given a certain independence. He goes to school, listens, and is given more general, and fewer specific directives. When twelve, the directives are still more general. When eighteen, still more confidence is placed in him. When twenty-one, a man has a relative independence in a normal situation. Religious obedience does not in any sense deny or destroy this relative independence. It is supposed to foster a mature independence which guides the religious toward the fuller observance of his Institute's general spirit. If a religious cannot understand the general spirit of his Institute, he should be dismissed, not simply confined in a jacket of specific rules. This applies to Superiors as well as subjects. Let him go elsewhere and employ his abilities before he is too old to adjust. If he shows that he understands something of the spirit of the Institute, he should be able to use an area of initiative. The founder wanted subjects to become adults. It is, of course, easy to govern children. Religious life, however, calls for adults.

QUESTION. "If *all* Christians are called to be perfect as our heavenly Father is perfect, why so much stress on perfection for religious?

ANSWER. When Christ called all men to be holy, he had all mankind in mind, not just religious. All men have an obligation to tend to the perfection of charity under the pain of mortal sin. Religious have a special way of deepening their baptismal consecration.

QUESTION. "I think we have exaggerated the importance of the 'religious life.' All Christians have been called to a perfect life. The only difference between me and my married sisters is that I chose to give my life in total dedication to service in the Church, in a different form of life. I did not receive any sacrament for that life. I simply had a conviction that I was called to it and the grace of a generous response. However, I have found myself buried under a mountain of trivial minutiae which seems to be the end-all of religious life. They are almost the end of me. My married sister has to be chaste in her sacramental marriage state. This leaves me with poverty and obedience. I think obedience means go where one is sent, do what one is told, but I do not think it means innumerable juvenile tasks that children do at home."

ANSWER. If the Superior insists upon innumerable juvenile commissions, he or she is juvenile. The founder or foundress did not intend that the organization should be so run. If he or she had, the Church would not have approved the constitutions. The Church has always shown great respect for human nature, as God Himself has. He made it. It is not the intention of God or the Church to destroy our humanity or our adulthood. If some misguided or ignorant Superiors administer an Institute so as to destroy adulthood, they are going *directly contrary to the call of the Spirit* in the Church. They are frustrating the will of God. They should be dismissed, at once.

QUESTION. "Poverty consists in the spirit in which I deny myself and is a personal thing."

ANSWER. Poverty also consists in obeying the rules of the Institute on poverty. The poverty of a Jesuit is different from that of the Franciscan Fathers, or the Carmelite Fathers, or the Dominican Fathers. It depends upon the spirit, the rules, and the constitution of the Order. It is not therefore entirely a personal thing. There are certain modifications dependent on our apostolate. If one is president of a college, it may be necessary to have a car. Someone else may be content with a bicycle. This variation in style of life is a function of the apostolate. The make of the car should fit with the spirit and mentality of one's vocation.

QUESTION. "It seems to me that religious should consider themselves a branch of the laity rather than some heavenly bush, mysterious and unknown, a bush, might I add, that is sometimes burned?"

ANSWER. Religious life is a particular evangelical form of life that the Church has approved. The basic question is: to what depth does each of us live the original insight of our group?

QUESTION. "Is there a rôle for the artist, the creative artist, the writer, in religious life?"

ANSWER. There certainly should be. It is true that religious who write fiction often feel they will have difficulty publishing it, that censors are unreasonably difficult. It is my hope that this will change. Some of the great prophetic voices of the Church, like Mauriac, Marcel, Greene, have been fiction writers. They place things in the concrete so as to bring home to ordinary men the basic problems. As regards art, organizers and administrators are not always willing to set aside people for art. They sometimes share an unchristian belief that art is a luxury. This is really a phase of a quite general question. There is a growing difference in the Church in religious life between a bureaucratic mold of action and a professional mold of action.

QUESTION. "Are not all religious at fault in that they tolerate the present situation where they are kept irresponsible children?"

ANSWER. We are all responsible for the situation that now obtains. We have sometimes preferred a type of security which is the security of the infantile. Religious, as a group, have not gently, but firmly, insisted on certain Christian truths. At times fears of reprisals and human prudence, the prudence of the flesh, have dictated that the best thing to do is to shut up and do as they are told. We have all contributed to the present situation. The young generation, however, seem to have tremendous devotion to honesty and to openness. Another generation had different values—a strong sense of obligation, of duty, and of collaboration. This generation has a conviction of personal responsibility to the Institute and to the group. That implies that at times they may openly express views that are unacceptable, but, by and large, they deserve admiration, a hearing, and our wholehearted support.

⊞ FIVE·AFFECTIVE LIFE AND PERSONALITY DEVELOPMENT

PASCAL SAID that one would have to be God to speak well of God. And to speak well of divine charity, one also needs the special grace of the Spirit. The virtue of charity is not an easy virtue either theoretically or practically. Described by theologians as the queen of all virtues, it is the archetypal virtue of Christianity, the central virtue of the Old Testament. Theologians speak of it as the form of all the virtues: any virtue without a relationship to charity is not authentic.

This subject ties together many of the topics previously discussed. Freedom in dialogue is necessarily connected with charity; one can conduct a monologue or a two-sided monologue without charity, but not a dialogue. Freedom, obedience, poverty, chastity—all relate to charity. If religious were more charitably concerned with persons, poverty would not pose so distressing a crisis today. Charity is closely connected with the questions we asked in our first chapter: is a religious habit or a religious symbol an armor against individuality? Charity is also related to the question of maturity since the mature individual is marked by an ability to give and to receive affection.

It is difficult to explain charity theoretically because a number of theoretical errors are widespread on this subject. That is not surprising. While man can easily grasp that he ought to love God, it is more difficult to see that he ought to love his neighbor and to love him as himself. That phrase *as oneself* is not at all a limiting phrase in the original text. Rather it suggests that we try to bring about an existential solidarity with our neighbor such as we have normally and naturally with our own interests. The Christian is invited to establish this solidarity with the interests of others by a victory over egotism. Charity thus involves a kind of *ex-stasis*, a standing outside oneself and making "the other" the center of one's personal existence. It is astonishing to many that Christ laid such emphasis on this virtue. It comes hard to human nature to believe that the ordinary human being whom we meet in every situation is a sacrament of Christ, the visible sign of the invisible Christ. Yet in Christian legend, the repository of many profound insights, this theme is a perennial one. Many find it difficult to take literally the description of the Last Judgment which accentuates so strongly the need for charity toward one's neighbor. The evangelist is not, of course, presenting charity there as the *exclusive* Christian virtue, but as its supreme absolute. We are supposed to cultivate other virtues also, but a prominence is given to charity which causes us to re-think certain of our fundamental human prejudices. The centrality of charity is also insisted upon by the mystics: St. John of the Cross insists that we shall be judged by love.

This selfless Christian love is not easily come by. It is hard for men to take Christ's commandment entirely seriously, for often they are tempted to feel that they would have arranged the moral order quite differently. Many might have put references to divine and positive law at the heart of the Christian theology of perfection. We may, however, assume in all intellectual tranquility that the Lord knew what He was doing, knew whereof He spoke.

It is extraordinarily painful to human nature to embrace

this great virtue when it touches certain raw issues: how is it possible to love one who has genuinely injured us with the intention of malice? Human nature rebels so strongly at this that nothing save a supernatural revelation would ever convince us that we have to. There are many caricatures of fraternal charity, pseudo-charities. The higher a virtue stands in the hierarchy of virtues, the more caricatures seem possible, the more pseudo-virtues flourish. St. Paul in his great hymn to charity (I Cor. 13) describes this virtue in its practical attitudes. John in his epistles insists on it with a strength of affirmation dismaying to us when we reflect on our own conduct. He says we know, we are assured, that we have been translated from death into life, and then ends with the phrase "because we love the brethren." Perhaps the ordinary Christian would be tempted to end it "because we love *God*." St. John insists also that if we do not abide in love, then we abide in death. This contrast of death and life, light and darkness, love and the lack of love is characteristic of John. From St. John we can be certain that, if we do not have this type of love for the brethren, we are not in the state of grace. This same insistent identification of grace and the presence of God with charity is seen in the liturgy.

In its biblical sense, grace is actually love. The ordinary Christian usually sees grace more as a kind of reified or objectified love of God for us. Grace, our new life in God, is a gift which manifests the existence within the Deity of a personal attitude toward us which we call love. The created gift of grace which we receive could not exist without the continued loving self-donation of the lover to us. Grace is a showing forth, an objectification, an incarnation, a reification of an inner personal attitude on the part of the Divinity, an attitude of love. Our fraternal charity requires that we imitate that love by a healthy love of ourselves, not to be identified with that brutal, pre-given existential solidarity with oneself which is egotism. This problem of genuine self-love and its nature preoccupied scholastics for centuries; it is not exactly easy to give a theoretical solution. At least we can say that we are required to love ourselves as persons, with the personal values we have, and to extend to ourselves, as persons, something of the same discretion, kindness, compassion, tolerance that we extend to other equally difficult human beings.

Charitable affection and warmth are necesary for the full development of the human person. The impoverishment of love of and in children, as previously discussed, results either in death or in a disturbance of the personality. This is true of adults, too. Man flourishes best, his creativity becomes more manifest and more easy, his energy is doubled, when he dwells in an atmosphere where he feels the normal currents of warm acceptance. If he receives genuine love from the brethren, his energy is likely to be tripled. Human beings, including religious, need a kind of erosphere if they are to survive as human beings. Man depends upon his atmosphere. If it is too rarefied, he reacts to it biologically and spiritually. There is a hot, dry wind which comes off the Sahara Desert and blows across Europe; it is called by various names: the "mistral" by the French, the "sirocco" by the Italians, the "fühn" by the Austrians. When this wind is blowing, crimes of violence are punished more mildly, for the wind affects the nerves, the minds, the emotions, the passions, and through them also the intelligence and free will of the individual. Even saints are affected by these conditions: St. Peter Canisius could not endure the *fühn*.

So also, in the psychological order, there is a need of a

favorable atmosphere for the human person to breathe as a human being: this atmosphere implies acceptance, love, and encouragement. His disciples accused St. John the Evangelist of speaking of nothing but this in his old age. According to legend, that was the only lesson that John saw fit to teach in his old age: "Little children, love one another." When his listeners complained about the scarcity of St. John's imagination as a pedagogue, he explained that his teaching represented authentic tradition on charity dating back to the Incarnate Word. Moral theology in the last twenty years has returned to that intuition. An ancient Christian insight is being brought to the fore again: there is no virtue unless it is connected with charity, and there is no vice except what is somehow opposed to charity. Charity is a decisive element in Christianity. It is not a minor virtue added to major virtues such as obedience, or chastity. Law, and obedience to law, are not the primary things in morality. The existence of affective, warm, familial charity is something for which all, including religious, constantly strive under pain of grave sin. At times, the existential novelists have brought this truth home to the theologian with more concreteness and force than theologians would have thought possible. The novels of Mauriac and Greene emphasize and re-emphasize this point. At times they emphasize it to distortion, as when they indulge in a kind of sin mystique, asserting that every great love creates its own laws, and if it be sinful, this is unimportant. Genuine charity is a great gift from God, and divinizes and humanizes the one who receives it. As far as the existentialist moralists' positive insights go, they are often quite right, for insofar as love is a victory over egotism, it is something to be treasured; but insofar as it is guilty, love is to be depreciated; it falls short of the authentic character of love.

The Christian has received strong intimations from Christ Himself that charity is part and parcel of His revelation of how man is humanized and divinized. Christ has insisted that we love our neighbor as ourselves. He has proclaimed that this love is a proof of the divinity of His Church. One may wonder whether the charity of the Church, and our own, has grown lukewarm, if our witness to charity does not make evident the divinity of the Church. The demand of Christ that we love our neighbor fits in with the nature of mankind as He made it. None of the commandments of Christ are extrinsic commandments imposed upon us to limit, in any way, our freedom; they are rather intended to broaden our freedom. Neither are they simply external directives as to how best to fulfill the will of God; they also have a "revealing" aspect: they reveal something to man about his own inner potentialities as a man. Consequently, they tend to expand man's human potentialities, not to suppress his humanity. Charity does this in a rather conspicuous fashion. It aims not only at the fulfillment of God's will, but also at man's own personal self-development. Man is most fully himself when he so possesses himself in freedom that he is capable of transcending himself to make a donation or gift of himself to another, either in the totality of his personality in marriage or in the totality of his energies, his warmth, his affectivity in consecrated virginity for the service of the Church. As God has fashioned man, man is related to others, essentially so; and if he is going to fulfill his own destiny as being human, he has to enter into a genuine community with others, a community based upon love, a warm, human, affectionate series of relationships. By love, Christ did not mean a bloodless, desubstantialized "I will do for him what I think is good for him, whether he wants it or not." The created personality is made an echo of the personality within the Trinity. In the Trinity, the Persons are sub-sistent relations; they stand toward others. They are altero-directed, not directed toward themselves. If the Christian—and the religious—is to live as human, he must manifest this same relational character. Religious, too, must be actually related to others in the relationship of love. He cannot live as an isolated unit within the Mystical Body because he was not brought into the Mystical Body as an isolated indi-vidual; he is a member of the body, a branch of the vine. He lives within a higher and transcendent unity which is itself living: the Mystical Body of Christ. A relational existence of warmth, of affective love is a precondition for being Chris-tian, for achieving human adulthood, and for functioning as a religious. If men were to sever these relations and live as depersonalized units, they would not be human beings. They would not long remain psychologically normal, and they would certainly not be full human beings, developed, ade-quate, complete. Nor would they be Christians.

That such is our nature may well have been discovered by natural reason reflecting upon the relationships which man's nature imposes upon him. It is, however, quite possible that men would never have arrived at a full, immediate, and clear understanding of what he is as a human being if Christ had not given this commandment to love one another. Man could have arrived at a great number of metaphysical truths by his reason, which he *de facto,* did not discover until God re-vealed them. One could have arrived at the notion of cre-ation by reason alone; *de facto,* man did not come to the idea of creation until it was revealed by God.

It is possible that, without Christ's revelation of this com-mandment to love, men would never have had the self-understanding that they have, or that deep sense of security that comes from an acknowledged unity with the entire people of God on march toward its final, corporate destiny.

On the natural level, too, man has to live in relationship if he is to perfect his personality. The greatest danger to natural personality is egotism, a closing-in on one's self, indigenous to one born in the state of original sin. Therefore, human adulthood may never have been so available as a living, concrete, existential possibility if Christ had not revealed His commandment to love. Christians, and religious, must always be aware that Christ uttered certain new words in the history of morality; we have to study them against this backdrop of the "first time," reflecting on Him and His mystery, for we have been used to them since our youth and may tend to take them for granted. The Christian commandment to charity is a startling new word in moral theory. The pre-Christian philosophers did not evolve even a sketch of this doctrine. The Stoic had some notion of the common unity of men, but one based upon such materialistic notions that we cannot consider it even a sketch of the new position Christ elaborated. As a result of His commandment, Christians today must be aware that insofar as a human being is closed, incommunicable, devoid of relationships of love, in just that proportion will he be unfulfilled, inhuman, and unchristian. It is not part of the Christian vocation to be inhuman. The existence of an individual is seriously impoverished if he is not established in relationships of love to others. If one lives in a depersonalized world of objects, a life becoming more common today, one lives in a world progressively less human and less Christian.

There is a mechanization of the human spirit that is a popular trend today: individuals, even in religious life, are sometimes considered as simply so many units, factors, ploys, counters, manipulative objects; men are dealt with as subjects capable of putting in so many hours of work per day, or gaining so much money a day, deriving so many ideas a day, or spending so much energy—they can also be considered a commodity to be bought and sold. It is for this reason that recent Popes have stressed so intensively the truth that man's work is a human thing, and that man himself is not simply an object capable of so much productivity. Theologians have tried to formulate a theology of work, to find out its meaning in a Christian situation.

Nonetheless, there is perennially present the temptation to ignore the personal world which is a completely unique world. That which is most perfect in the whole creation is the human person, says St. Thomas. Christians, too, and religious, are tempted to evade this personal world, or to ignore it; if they do enter it, they deal with it as though it responded to the same laws to which matter responded: the law of force. Laws of force are operative not only in obvious, external, material pushes and pulls, but also in the psychological pressures exerted upon individuals. These are pressures from the sociological situation in which man lives, pressures from the community, economic pressures, pressures to conformism, pressures of manipulation. Those who know how to shape the urges of men are able to exploit these urges by the use of fear, greed, and other depersonalizing pressures. These signs are evidence of our fundamental temptation to disregard the existence of that completely unique dimension of reality, the personal dimension.

A trend not uncommon today in a universe partly secularistic is to treat the other, not as though he had an inner subjectivity to which I must respond, but as though he were something out there, pre-given, a kind of object in a field of force. The person then becomes something to be coped with, manipulated, exploited, avoided, destroyed, rendered harmless. Such attitudes can, of course, influence even "religious" men. If that tendency is allowed to grow, a man may indeed deal effectively in a subhuman universe; but he cannot deal with another in a human, Christian, religious way. If I am to enter into a union or a dialogue with another, I have to acknowledge the fact that this other has an inner subjectivity and an open destiny, a destiny open to the infinite. I must acknowledge secondly that he has his own personal and unrepeatable individuality which must be respected. Each man and each religious possesses a personal law of progress written into his being which I cannot violate. I cannot skip over organic stages even to help a person to be "better" or brighter or more educated or more docile. A religious attitude rather respects the type of rhythm characteristic of this individual. If I am to be human and Christian in dealing with the other, I have to collaborate with the inner themes spoken by God in this individual, and not to be repeated.

Christian charity demands an insight, a humanism, a "benignity and humanity" which is not always characteristic of Christians or religious men. Observing what the other's God-given themes are, *his* inner potentialities for expansion as a human being, I must grant him a spiritual freedom, an atmosphere favorable to these themes so that they may unfold as they are in him, not as I have predecided they should be unfolded or not as I would have done had I been the creator. "If I am not I," Thoreau wrote, "who else will be?" Or can be, we may add. I must respect the *I am* of my neighbor if I am to be *I am*, too. Individuals must be allowed organically to unfold the word that the Lord has spoken in them.

Therefore, the commandment of Christ that we should love one another suggests to us that we try to enter into an open and barrierless communion, a defenseless, vulnerable openness to the other. At the same time charity demands an intimate respect for what God has done in the other. Man, then, needs spiritual space to unfold. This requires that any interpersonal block between the two be demolished so that we can achieve this. Pull down the stockades! Cross the interpersonal space between two! This is not always done even in the best religious communities; religious often live in polite estrangement. Christians are called upon to establish a community of insight, a we-ness with the other, not precisely a frontal I-Thou relation, but a lateral we-relationship directed to common projects. Christ ordained His Church to be an open communion of all men; within that Church, each little community that is Christian should have the same logos: "organized love." The *adjective* is "organized." The noun carries the weight: it is *love*, or *agape*, disinterested *love*. If such open communion is not had, inevitably there will exist insecurity, distresses, manifested perhaps physiolgically in headaches, psychosomatic symptoms, or in boredom, disinterestedness, withdrawal, or other neurotic symptoms. What Christ intended for the Church, and for religious communities, mirrors of the Church, is a communion, an *open* communion. The communion of saints on earth objectively establishes Christians as a group with an élan for and toward and forward to the beatific vision; the beatific vision is clearly not a group of unrelated individuals staring at an "object." God is a personal

God; and the joy of Heaven is not the sum of the disparate joys of disparate individuals, but the unity of all men come to their term, facing the Lord, supremely open to him and to one another. This unity of all men in Christ is pre-reflected here on earth in the Church; it should be so reflected in a religious community. The more we are unable to enter into the intimate spirit of the community, a spirit of openness, barrierlessness, defenselessness, readiness to encounter the others, to meet in a genuine, mutual accessibility and availability, the less Christian, the less religious we are. We are then also more impoverished as purely human beings.

Jesus Christ revealed himself particularly in the warmth of His love and His concern, His compassion for the multitude, His ability to enter into the states of soul of others; He then revealed Himself as the supreme exemplar of our human nature. He reveals, in His charity, that human nature has depths and potentialities it suspects fully only in contact with Him. The philosophic insight that man is so established by nature that he cannot fulfill himself without relatedness, has become a part of Christian culture even shared by the atheist; after one has abandoned Christianity, one may keep its cultural values. Man frustrates himself at his deepest level as person and as Christian if he insists upon living as an isolated individual.

Christ "informs" all our human loves, that is to say, He imposes upon them a new perfection. He divinizes them; He also hierarchizes them so that we do not love Beethoven or Bach more than God. Whenever a value is displaced from its God-ordained position in the hierarchy of values, it is not exalted even if this be the intention, but demeaned. Christ gives us a hierarchy for our loves. At the same time He gives them a new form: He divinizes them. He suppresses absolutely nothing authentic in human love. This is something which we must never weary of explaining to those who do not understand the Christian vocation: whatever type of love exists, if it be authentic love, a victory over egotism and selfishness, it will find its ultimate fulfillment only in the Christ. For this reason philosophers have pointed out that every great natural love, no matter how intense, powerful, sacrificial, and noble it may be, is, to a certain extent, unfulfilled, limited, destined to frustration if it is not a love in the Christ. Every great love tends to go to the infinite in the direction of benevolence, in the conferring of gifts, and in the direction also of union. But neither of these inner tendencies of natural love can be fulfilled outside the Christ who is the objectively infinite gift we can confer upon another, the One who holds the ultimate secret to the beloved's personality and, consequently, the ultimate key to union.

Christ gives the religious a structure by which to hierarchize affections so that these do not enter into conflict one with the other. Man has many loves in his life, not all of the same type. These interpersonal relationships are given by Christ a hierarchy proper to them, so that man can locate them in the scale of preference and value. Christ, instead of desiccating our humanity, intends to intensify that humanity. So also with the entire affective sphere; to be without affectivity is not an ideal of Christianity. Such a chill life would be inhuman, depersonalized, and hence could not be divinized. The only thing that God can divinize is what He made: humanity. He cannot act upon men effectively as anything but men. It is His intention to intensify human nature and human love. Marriage in Christ is more intense in the *experiential* order than it is without Him; friendship in Christ is more intense on the experimental and experiential,

existential level than it is without Christ, as St. Aelred remarked many centuries ago.

A religious must have regard for Christ's commandment of
love in all its human and personal implications. Explanations
of the virtue of charity have been given which tend to muti-
late the human personality. Having regard to what centuries
of wisdom and experience have distilled for us in the instructions of moralists, friendship, love, is still a central Christian
value and must be cultivated, not feared. To assure a practical good, one cannot destroy a theoretical truth, lest one
end up in a morass of errors. When Christ calls upon us to
humanize, divinize, and hierarchize our loves, He seizes
upon every authentic affection as it exists in a concrete, historical, individual person, brings it into unity, and divinizes
it. Under no aspect does He distort our humanity or dimin-
ish it. Fraternal charity intensifies all legitimate affections.
There is consequently nothing contrary to the law of Christ
in being a kindly, warm-hearted, affectionate person. Christians are expected, as witnesses to this new breath which
Christ has brought into our existence, to bear witness to His
divinity by familial love. To do so, they need not, of course,
abandon discretion or intelligence. At times charity and love
are explained in such a fashion that one would think only he
could love universally who had abandoned his intelligence.

Charity does not require us to put up with every type of
selfishness. If there is only enough food here for two, and my
companion insists upon eating all, I will intervene to make
sure that I have sufficient for myself. As long as I intervene
sensibly and graciously, and with warmth and affection,
there is absolutely nothing against charity. We must recall
also that the command of Christ to fraternal charity is not a
juridical fiction. At times charity is explained very much as

though the Lord said to us: "Let us both play a game. You pretend, and I'll pretend. You pretend that the neighbor is Christ, and I'll pretend that you are fulfilling something that is natural and normal to your personality in loving Him." No. If Christ tells us to treat other men as though they were Christ, there must be truth in this order; it cannot be an external order imposed upon us bearing no relation to the real state of affairs. Christ does not order us to perfection by means of deceits; if He tells us that in a realistic sense the neighbor is Christ, the sacramental Christ, this must be true. Occasionally, His commandment to love is explained as though one should ignore the real lovability in the other and treat him "as if" he were Christ. "As if" . . . I submit that this is not the wish of Christ. What we must do is to reach the depth in the other at which we encounter the Christ who *de facto* is there.

Charity does not suggest to us that we substitute for the warm living breath of love an impersonal, detached, anti-septic case-worker technique, a technique of kindness and understanding or even genuine service. Service is not a sub-stitute for love; service may be the fruit of love, but if it is given without love, it is not Christian service. Any technique of kindness, thoughtfulness, consideration, service to another, which is devoid of personal commitment, of personal in-volvement with the other, is not fully Christian. One cannot so easily do the work of God with detached hands. The reli-gious is not called to love others by prescinding from whether they are lovable or not; he is called to love them because they have within them genuine lovability. When we cannot see that too easily, we can reflect on this: being is a transcendental; hence, that one exists means that there is some good in him: *omne ens bonum*.

Christians must search for the lovability in others and strive to find the living Christ in others. Charity is in no sense based upon a juridical fiction. Since men are the children of God, they may be loved as such; they may be also loved for their natural gifts, good reasons for loving. But men can be loved for their supernatural gifts, sanctifying grace and the theological virtues and the attendant moral gifts. Even that is not the final explanation of charity. The difficulty with the "as if" theory is this: the person who acts on that concept of charity is doing exactly the opposite of what Christ ordained that he should do. What Christ ordained is that man should love men as well as God. What the "as if" theory accomplishes is a bypassing of men to love God the more securely. This involves an implicit denial of the defined dogma of the Incarnation. It is undeniable that such approaches may result in some lateral ethical good, but they involve a basic misunderstanding of the essential nature of fraternal charity, a commandment of the highest ethical import. One does not need to bypass the human to love the divine more securely, because we are forbidden by the Lord Himself to treat men as a means to an end. Men have within themselves an irreducible value to which we must respond objectively. Even if a man's purpose or end be to love God more, he still can not use others as a means to that end. The likelihood is that a man, in the "as if" theory, will end in neither loving man nor loving God, since he will not fulfill the primal commandment of God, charity. Charity implies love, and not an instrumentalization of the other even for the achieving of some "moral" goal.

Through the creative goodness of God, each man has within himself a natural goodness of existence. He has a unique value. He holds it and possesses it as his, his invitation to the divine, his destiny, and it is this the Lord has suggested we look for in humanity. If man responds to the dignity found in the other, then, as a gift, there will flow back to him, by a metaphysical law of superabundance, an increase in moral goodness. That increase will only be achieved if it is not directly striven for by instrumentalizing others to increase my moral virtue.

Man is moreover commanded by God to love, not only the natural and supernatural gifts that God has given to our neighbor, but also to search out the living Christ within our neighbor. How can he do that? He can, because fraternal charity is a theological virtue, a divine virtue. Charity is a theological virtue, because man's motive for loving the other is the Lord, God; He is the reason we love the other. Moreover, the Lord actually dwells within the other. If the other has the gift of grace, then he has within his soul that which is reflective of God in His Inmost Being. The entire nature of grace demands that it include the presence of the divine giver; it cannot be communicated, as other gifts are communicated, *in absentia*. For man to be graced, the loving God must be present to him. The Giver must bring His gift. Consequently, grace not only reflects God, but it also involves God's presence; wherever grace is present, God is specially present. In loving the individual who is "in the state of grace," one can actually reach through this concrete individual personality to the Lord who communicates Himself to him, impresses Himself upon this individual's soul. As a result, one cannot treat the other as a function by which he may arrive at God, a passive channel by which he may attain God. He should rather address his love to what is most individual in each person. Charity directs itself precisely at what is most individual, most personal, most incommunicable, most unique. This is true because, in metaphysical terms, that which is most profoundly personal in the individual is his incommunicable unique act of existence, the metaphysical root of personality, that which makes him to be himself and closes off the possibility of his becoming *part* of another. This act of existence is, however, continually poured into the other by the living God, present to him. Hence what makes each man unrepeatable, most personal, most human, is the continued creation, by the Lord, of this personal act of existence. At the depths of any man, there always stands Another, God, supplying to him the act of personality. This is true even in the purely natural order.

Hence it is God who holds the ultimate secret of each individual's personality, who knows the inner meaning of the pattern of existence He has given to each man; He is ever-present, acting, communicating existence to the individual. In loving this individual, the Christian loves what is most concrete, unrepeatable, individual in him, all the shades of his personality. He also then encounters the Lord God within man, communicating the act of existence, sustaining each one's unique personality in existence. In a genuine, philosophical sense, what we love in any person is the highest and most dense concentration of his individuality, his *I am*. But if one touches that uttermost individuality, one finds there the Lord sustaining that personality in its uniqueness, His *I Am*.

If the above is true in the natural order, how much more so in the supernatural order where one finds in man not only the Creator God, but also the self-donating God. In the graced soul, one meets the Trinity donating Itself to this soul at its depth, forming, quasi-actuating, the soul. The God of grace is newly present in an individual in the state of grace;

we discover Him present there as the form of this form, if you will, of the soul of this soul, fused with it as fire is fused with iron thrown into the fire: the indwelling God is constantly impressing Himself there.

Christian charity in its ultimate meaning is theandric; it is incarnate, both human and divine; it intensifies what is human in us and it enables us also to love with a vigor, fire, clemency, and constancy which is divine. It is most intensely human because it appreciates, as no natural humanist can appreciate, all the humanity of the other; it reaches to the ultimate last depths of that individuality and to the living God who sustains it. It is divine because we love, within the individual, Him who sustains him in being and, if he is in the state of grace, Him who communicates Himself in an utterly mysterious union, in an indescribable intimacy.

God is present in the neighbor not as an inert thing, but as One who forms the conscience of the other, renders the other susceptible to open communion. He is One who enables the isolated individual to have the courage, the security, to break down both barriers and natural securities and to enter into a genuine, open community. It would be a distorted, impoverished approach to fraternal charity that would empty it of all genuine love, believing that one makes God the motive of our love for a person simply because of a command. It is because the Lord is *in* the other individual that we are able, by the new, expanded intelligence given in faith, to find Christ within the neighbor. If we are to accept Christ's moral revolution with any realism, we must not empty it of ontological meaning, of basic realism. We cannot translate it into some kind of a fairy story, as though Christ, the substantial revelation of God and the bearer of the divine message, were deceiving us when He told us that the neighbor is to be loved. If He so instructed us, it is because charity falls in with our human nature and expands it to its total reference.

Christian love is, of course, realistic. It is aware of the differences between charity and such aberrations as sentimentality or veiled self-seeking or sensuality. A Pollyanna approach to reality, an approach that denies men can be difficult, is not endorsed. It would be a very peculiar kind of divine commandment which dehumanized humanity or substituted for man's natural warmth and affection something desubstantial, bloodless. It is not the intention of the Incarnate God to suppress humanity in man, but to divinize it. Therefore religious, in loving men for a supernatural motive, must also love with a warm, human affection, as God commanded. Within the ambit of our possibilities, religious men and women must love universally—this does not imply that we love all the same way or to the same degree. That would be unrealistic because all are not the same: a child is not an old man; Peter is not John. Christians have to love within the limits of their ability to understand and to accept men. To attempt to love all "equally," as some ascetical writers used to suggest, usually meant an attempt to love no one at all. Nor does a religious take the small amount of affection that he could have given to one person and spread this thin over everyone. That is obviously not what the Lord hoped for.

All Christians must cultivate openness and readiness to enter into human relations, but they cannot understand all men to the same degree. Readiness to foster the inner values of each, to collaborate with the inner theme of the other and to render ourselves accessible in mutual availability to the other is the work of the religious man. If we do that, then we

expand because there is a constant expanding of our contact
with humanity; and, in each of these new contacts, there is
that which confirms me in my security and aids the expansion of my own personality. This type of charity is much less
easy than the standard misinterpretations. Many religious
think that charity is easy; to those, I suggest that they try
it. Often they substitute for genuine warmth and affection a
kind of natural, easy, superficial *bonhommie* which does not
imply divine charity. There can be substituted for charity
an *egotism à beaucoup*, small groups based upon natural
sympathies, inclinations, or interests. These never imply love
unless they demand a victory over egotism. Love never exists
unless there is an *ex-stasis*, where we place the other, as far
as we can, in the hierarchy of our loves, at the center of our
existence in place of ourselves. Charity demands renouncement. It demands continual humility and mortification, especially if we are to open to those who do not naturally
attract us.

There is no advantage to perfection in being deprived of
love or in failing to love. If the life of a consecrated religious
manifested normally less conquest over selfishness, less genuine love than did the married state, it would not be a more
perfect form of life. Any form of life which limits man's
capacity to love is not Christian. The lack of a partner of the
opposite sex can be an occasion for many dangers, and unfortunate psychological developments. If the fulfillment
which nature brings to the married person is missing for the
unmarried, piety will not suffice as a substitute. The unmarried man often does not have the experience which stimu-
lates him to define himself humanly. He does not have one
who gives him the experienced reality of security and support, one whose talents and attitudes provide both a correc-

tive and complement for his own. The unmarried woman
does not have one who can awaken her inner life, takes her
completely as she is, to whom she can look for shelter and
encouragement, while opening him to his individuality.

Unmarried men and women avoid a number of dangers,
but they are faced with sharp problems of their own. Where
these problems are not faced, unfortunate psychological developments can result; an unmarried religious can be
domineering, ambitious, arctic, isolated, or he can be effem-
inate, sentimental, interiorly uncertain, timid, scrupulous,
withdrawn, moody, unloving.

Among the unfortunate developments for the unmarried is
the search for "love" in some inferior substitute. A religious
can "sublimate" his basic desire for love in some other preoccupation: food, money or, more dangerous, power. I remember that, when I was walking through Rome's streets
one day, an old lady asked me, "Padre, padre, please give me
something; I am blind." I said, "Then tell me, how did you
know I was a padre?" "Well," she answered, "you were talking about food."

There are clerics who draw women to themselves under
the transparent guise of spiritual direction: they have their
flock of mystic, admiring doves, a spiritual seraglio, if not a
hierarchic harem. The unmarried woman is especially close
to some woman friend or concentrates her love on her employer; a nun pours forth her love on her Superior. In all, an
unconscious instinct works to win some individual for one's
self. These dangers threaten the existence of genuine religious communities; priests and religious are more and more
choosing to live outside communities which are unloving.
Even the person who had dedicated himself or herself to
God cannot do without human partners; human partnership

belongs to human life as such. This partnership does not mean marital love or its expressions, but persons with whom God brings a religious in contact should be loved. Everyone must undertake the risks of love, with its joys and its disappointments; if one doesn't, he is not human. Love is indispensable, the unique effective school of selflessness. The possibilities range here from a life in a community, supposed to be organized love, up to and including friendship, a moral good, no matter what pious books have said.

Common life, which often accompanies religious celibacy, is both a schooling and a testing of genuine love—at least, it should be. Religious formation does not always explain common life as having anything to do with love, but Christian celibacy or common, religious life is the sharing of love, not its absence. If it is not, it is not authentic celibacy or virginity. More and more Christians are noting this today. There must be truth to it; when people from all over the world of varying minds, formations, philosophic backgrounds, theological backgrounds, say the same thing, there is a suggestion that the Spirit is speaking. Openness to God demands openness to men, openness not merely in the abstract, but in the confrontation with individual persons. If it is true, as has been often said, that religious are most reluctant ever to engage in confrontation, something has gone wrong in their formation; if religious are incapable of genuine encounter, something has gone very wrong: their life, then, is antichristian.

Decisive for the flowering and fruitfulness of virginity is the union a religious finds in love with God, but one cannot be united with God until one is united with man. For him to whom the supernatural world is real, there will be pangs at the renunciation of married love; but the heart is fuller than

it could be from human association because one is associated with God and with all His human family.

Are there many dedicated to chastity who live in the
world of the pseudo-spiritual, and not enough in the every-
day world where adventures of love are possible? The great
saints were able to combine both worlds. This is the reason
their love was so luminous. The great saints were very often
humanists in their approach to reality.

Today we note that many religious seek outside the religious life, the family atmosphere, the love which they do not
find in their community. Why do they not find it in their
community? The atmosphere in the community, some maintain, is too cool, too unconcerned with the needs of the individual. If this is true, then the community is at fault; if there
is no real community, all should move out and live as Christians, not as frauds playing the game of religion. Some cut
themselves off from the community or even seek to withdraw from it completely, yet all those whom God has called
to an unmarried life have a great obligation to encourage
community life and the family spirit. Family life among religious, and community spirit, does not mean "least common
denominator" charity, where all differences are dissolved in
a dishonest peace, and authentic issues never discussed;
rather it means a real confrontation, a real encounter, a real
openness, even where there are differences. This concerns
not only religious Orders and congregations, but also dioce-
san priests. Religious should not merely make demands upon
the community, but rather contribute to the community, so
that a brotherly spirit comes into being. One who does this
in a genuine community overcomes the dangers involved in
renouncing the family; if the community supplies the affection, the support, the warmth that the religious individual

needs, if upon leaving one brother he finds a thousand, there will be fewer dangers to chastity, fewer who go mad, or become psychotic or neurotic or bitter. Fewer will leave. Religious cannot live in a loveless atmosphere and flourish. Who can? No one is called to, by Christ; quite the opposite, all are called to, as each is called to, as Christ Himself was called to—and did—love.

Negative renouncement can be converted into positive acquisition; freedom from the cares of a family can make one free for the cares of all. Here is the heart of the call to consecrated virginity. He who wishes to belong to God must be willing to belong to man. Nothing frees a man from insecurity and the feeling of being alone as does concern for others. The man always concerned for others is forever fashioning for himself new security.

There are many who, precisely because they are unmarried, for the sake of the Kingdom of Heaven, have matured into selfless love; God has given them a new fruitfulness as fathers and mothers of a great family. If religious look upon the whole area of renunciation with its attendant dangers, they must conclude that it is a lofty and rewarding thing, but one difficult and painful. If concrete conditions render it impossible, a person should not attempt it; it is a task that, humanly speaking, is impossible of accomplishment.

What ideally should be the character of love in the religious life? It should be something like that love which exists in a good, normal, happy family. There, differences of age, differences of convictions, differences of training, differences of personality are accepted. We accept these things and we accept them within the framework of a previous acceptance of the *person*. Is human love possible in religious life? If religious life is devoid of human love, it is not religious life or Christian life: it is sinful anarchy; it is not religious. Certainly it is not life; it is death. St. John notes that: moral death.

QUESTION. "It seems to me that many saints were capable of deeply human love."

ANSWER. The saints were very loving people, not only toward the Lord Himself, but toward all with whom they dealt. They also had personal friends. St. Theresa of Avila was not the least holy of women, and yet she had dear personal friends. Even men! Nonetheless she is canonized. So also, St. Francis de Sales and Jeanne de Chantal.

There is a beautiful book by St. Aelred on holy friendship, and there is an excellent theological article by Von Steenherghen in the *Dictionnaire de Spiritualité* entitled "friendship," "amitié."

QUESTION. "Is not human love just one other means to an end—total consecration to and love of God?"

ANSWER. The two go hand in hand: one is not a means to the other. One cannot go to God by bypassing God. God has, by His own free choice, become incarnate for all eternity. We must believe that there was a wisdom about this. If He joins Himself to His Church in the union of love symbolized by marriage, then man must love humanity. We can, however, only love humanity properly insofar as we love God. That is the motive for our love for humanity. We can only love God insofar as we love humanity. To paraphrase St. John: "What is the point in saying you love God whom you do not see, when you do not love your neighbor whom you do see?" John also remarks rather bluntly that the man who says that he loves God, but does not love his brother, is a liar. I agree with St. John.

QUESTION. "But is not service the best proof of love? Should not we judge our love by our deeds?"

ANSWER. One cannot substitute loveless service for love. One can do all the services in the world, and they would irritate, if they do not come signed and formed with that discretion which only genuine love can give. Service is indiscreet otherwise; it offends and humiliates, while puffing up the "server."

Sanctity is measured eventually by *affective* love, by internal love, not by service. That is hard to measure. When the Church canonizes someone, she looks at what he did because this gives some indication of his internal love of God and man.

QUESTION. "Do not certain 'social service' vocations lay a heavier emphasis on love by service then on love of union?"

ANSWER. Yes. They should correlate the two more theologically.

QUESTION. "Is genuine personal love actually feasible among religious?"

ANSWER. It is possible. It should become more frequent. It is an ideal. One must, of course, understand the nature of interpersonal love, which is not a grasping sensuality, *egotism à deux*, or lust. Wherever the voice of lust sounds in the ear, immediately the call to love is dead: these two voices are incompatible. Interpersonal love is not sentimentality, not exclusivity, not childishness, not a regression to the infantile, such that one cries for mama or papa, Superiors or Superior. Genuine love is certainly possible for religious as long as they are Christians. Religious are not exempt from the fundamental, primal commandment of Christianity because they are dedicated to perfection!

QUESTION. "It seems to me that the ordinary explanation of chastity as love implies that religious universalize their charity by spreading a little love very thin over a great multitude, instead of concentrating it on a few."

ANSWER. If this were true, it would be better to marry.

QUESTION. "Does religious training at times invite us to a polite way of life that is really nothing but a mask, with little genuine confrontation?"

ANSWER. This has been charged very often. Perhaps religious do find it difficult to give themselves to others and to reveal their true selves. If this were universal—undoubtedly it is true in some cases—it would seem to manifest a lack of humility and also a great lack of self-respect and Christian self-love.

If a person does not have respect for himself and love for himself, he cannot be open with others. He can do all sorts of services while remaining a closed, opaque personality. Some people seem to have taken opacity as a Christian ideal. Whence they derive this notion, I do not know. Certainly not from Christianity! Some take it as an ideal that no one should know them and that they should reveal themselves to no one, should give themselves to no one, should live in an affective vacuum. That is not asceticism; it is simply a psychological deformation and an escape from Christian commitment. It is the perfect antithesis to Christianity.

QUESTION. "Is married love or the love of friendship the most authentic form of charity?"

ANSWER. If love is formed from within by selfless charity, and married love has a built-in invitation to this—and this is precisely the way God draws married people to sanctity— we may say that married love and religious life are two differing forms of charity.

QUESTION. "As religious grow older, it seems they tend to retract the circle of their friends, until, in old age, many end up utterly alone."

ANSWER. It seems a sign of maturity to expand one's circle of friends rather than retract it. Louis Beirnaert, the French Jesuit psychiatrist, points that out as one of the dominant tests of maturity. Religious who grow old and cannot make friends may well be becoming less mature as they age. Is the fault theirs or the Institute's?

QUESTION. "It seems humanly inevitable that there be real divisions in a community between, let us say, the bright and the less bright, the intellectuals and the artists and the apostles."

ANSWER. An intellectual or an artist can be an apostle too. Some artists are also athletes and intellectuals. Even where they aren't, there should be areas where they can communicate with others if they are members of a genuine community. There must be some interest in the life of an athlete besides athletics, otherwise he would not be in a religious community. The same is true of the artist, the intellectual. To have warmth and charity, we do not need to have agreement on ideas. Many dear, close friends disagree violently on politics and ideas. Communication is a communication to the person as a whole—I accept this person as a whole and would do anything possible to foster his values.

QUESTION. "To what extent does the training given to religious serve as a help or a hindrance in forming friendships with fellow religious and neighbors?"

ANSWER. At times a formation may be a hindrance, in that young people are inhibited from open communion with one another. For example, if there are no open discussions, but only a Superior talking at individuals, if individuals never form a body with one another and never confront one another face to face, if they are not trained to service and love, then their training is a hindrance to perfection. There have also been some extremely stupid things written on the subject of fraternal love.

QUESTION. "What are the causes of loneliness in the religious community?"

ANSWER. Very often it is the opacity we spoke of. Individuals have been trained to be of service to others, but not to be "with" them.

If anyone in the group will fix my window shade, but none will give me a word of encouragement or none will ever be open to me, I then live in a world of depersonalized robots. I will become uncomfortable after a while and eventually lonely. This is a problem which agitates young religious more and more. It seems to some incomprehensible that religious complain of the loneliness of religious life. What are the causes of this strange phenomenon? Malformation, failure in training toward charity and community, perhaps also psychological inadequacies in those accepted.

QUESTION. "What elements might help to solve this problem?"

ANSWER. Further study of the whole nature of community life is badly needed. How do we live it today? In what sense is this group of religious a community?

QUESTION. "How serious a danger to charity is the formation of cliques?"

ANSWER. That question answers itself. Closed-in groups where the outsider is not welcome are no part of an open community.

QUESTION. "What apostolic witness value does charity have for the individual in the Church?"

ANSWER. Christ Himself has answered that question. Christ wanted charity. He said it was a sign of His Church: by this shall all men know you are My disciples, because you love one another. This is still true; and if Christians have not had the influence in the world that they should have, perhaps the primary reason is this: we have been defective in love. Faith is generated, as modern theologians insist, not by intellectual debate, but by loving witness. A man who bears witness to his state—and how better can he bear witness to it than by living the first commandment of Christ of genuine selfless charity—is likely to draw others to belief. If religious vocations are rarer, if we are not much of a sign lifted up among the nations, it is that individually and collectively we have failed in deep preoccupation with the poor, with those whose rights are not recognized, with the disinherited. The disinherited can also be very wealthy, but disinherited spiritually, or psychologically, or intellectually. If religious fail to make an impact on the world, this is one of the chief reasons.

QUESTION. "Is a deep personal love between two individuals of the opposite sex compatible with the vows of chastity?"

ANSWER. Yes.

QUESTION. "I do not mean platonic love or spiritual love, but one involving the whole person."

ANSWER. Deep personal love between two individuals of the opposite sex is perfectly compatible with the vow of chastity. The question is: what is the nature of the love. If the nature of the love has those marks of exclusivity, face-to-face confrontation, an I-to-thou union, involving an immanent tendency to express that love in marital acts, it is marital love, not suitable for the religious.

QUESTION. "Is being safe of greater importance than taking a risk to love?"

ANSWER. No, it is of less importance. But the risks should be carefully avoided. When spiritual authors speak of the risks of love, they do not mean putting oneself in imprudent situations. That is not desirable. Of course, one cannot withdraw from every other human being in order to be safe. To be safe that way is to be dead, personally and spiritually. On the other hand, one has to follow the moral norms laid down for prudence in human situations.

QUESTION. "Donald Campion in *The Catholic Mind* has said: 'Those in authority must furnish an example of candor. There should be institutionalized guarantees of free and fearless opinion about authority's teachings and its prescriptions.' "

ANSWER. That is correct. The institutionalization of guarantees will be difficult to accomplish. But that is what religious must attempt. Such guarantees must be written into the law, and then we must see that there are means for enforcing the law. Those who disregard such guarantees should be punished. Candor is absolutely necessary.

QUESTION. "Who goes to the doctor—a Sister physically or mentally ill, or her Superior. Many Sisters are unable to communicate with their doctor because they know the Superior has made appointments, given her personal version of the symptoms, the case history, and so forth."

ANSWER. That is a violation of privacy. Normally speaking, an adult should go to the doctor by herself.

QUESTION. "Are there no limits to the authority of a Superior in private, personal areas of religious life?"

ANSWER. I do not know about Sisters, but I know normal men would impose limits quite quickly if Superiors pried into private matters.

QUESTION. "General suggestions as to the boundaries of the authority of Superiors, and the rights of the patient, will be appreciated."

ANSWER. A person doesn't give up all his rights to privacy when he enters the religious live. A Superior shouldn't pry into everything, especially if the doctor is a psychiatrist.

QUESTION. "Is there any connection between corporate poverty and social justice? For example, is corporate poverty involved when a community engaged in hospital work resists paying a living wage?"

ANSWER. Many religious do not feel that they have to obey the natural moral law. The commandment to pay just wages falls on religious just as well as on those in business. In certain cases, there may be a kind of tacit agreement on the part of those who work for religious to work for less. Where their employees want to be paid just wages, religious must pay them.

QUESTION. "Ultimately, of course, a religious community will be forced to conform to justice, but what of the scandal of those who resist social justice to the last ditch?"

ANSWER. It is a scandal. If religious can't operate a hospital or school efficiently enough to pay normal wages, they ought to get out and let in people who can operate it efficiently.

QUESTION. "Is corporate poverty involved when a community running large hospitals fails to organize buying for the institutions in the same city. Statistics show that hundreds of thousands of dollars are saved with such corporate buying. Would not our obligation to the poor make it mandatory to save all the money we can, the more effectively to serve them?"

ANSWER. This is not so much a question of poverty, but of common sense. I do not understand why religious wouldn't organize central buying. It would seem to be in accordance with common sense and prudence and poverty to do so.

QUESTION. "The term *sociological Catholicism* has been applied to some religious gestures which have become merely social rites. It seems that many of the so-called 'holy customs' of religious communities can be listed under the above caption. No one, not even the oldest members of the community, knows or appreciates their significance, but since we have always observed them, we continue to observe them."

ANSWER. That, I think, is an absolutization of pseudo-traditions. Meaningless customs should be eliminated immediately. That kind of ritual Catholicism may have had significance for another period of history. Such customs may be completely out of conformity with our present democratic epoch. They do not then provoke the inner attitudes that they once provoked. They are no longer effective symbols. Such an alienation of symbol from reality is visible where nuns genuflect in front of a Superior each time they meet her. A number of those antique customs, beautiful as they may have been in another period of history, should be dropped quietly, but rapidly—preferably yesterday rather than tomorrow.

QUESTION. "Comment please on 'particular friendships', a topic which seems a Jansenistic cudgel to suppress warm relationships between religious. Is it wrong to have one or two religious friends to whom one opens one's heart, whose presence one especially enjoys even though one loves all the community?"

ANSWER. No. It would be ideal if one could open his or her heart to all the community instead of to one or two. "Particular friendships" rather means those friendships which are destructive of the unity of the community. A friendship would be wrong if two who open their hearts to one another are unconcerned with the rest of the community, fail to take part in community exercises, recreation, or fail to share their joys with the community. If they create a little group of insiders who criticize others in the community, God is not in their midst. A "particular friendship" may mean also a homosexual relationship, latent or overt. Those distinctions having been made, we must add that normal friendship is a good thing in community life. Young people have to be trained to express their affection in a religious fashion, not in an irreligious fashion. As people grow into maturity, they should be able to have many genuine friendships within religious life. Some authorities do not agree with me on that, but it remains true.

QUESTION. "If such emphasis is put on the dangers of particular friendships, will religious be able to act as human beings?"

ANSWER. Masters and mistresses of novices who suppress humanity should be suppressed. We have to become human to be good Christians.

QUESTION. "Does the community fail in poverty when it has a policy of appointing Sisters who have personality difficulties to graduate study, without giving them any goal or community plan?"

ANSWER. I would have no objection to the community so spending its money, even if the Sister has a personality difficulty. Hopefully, she will come back more useful to the community. This may also be less expensive than giving her psychiatric care—or giving the whole community psychiatric care!

QUESTION. "I have a question concerning Catholic education. I agree that there are too many Catholic colleges and not all of high quality. But I question the view that priests have no place in higher education."

ANSWER. It was not my intention to suggest that no priest should ever be in education. On the contrary, I think that many of them should be. Nor do I think that Newman Centers are an adequate substitute for a Catholic education. I think there should be Catholic centers at universities in which a group of priests staff a center and teach on the university faculty of philosophy, theology, or the humanities.

The intellectual apostolate is a constant role in the Church. I question a certain practical form of it. Should we have the number of Catholic colleges that we have today? Should we not rather consolidate them and raise the quality of education? Is this not a matter of justice?

▟ SIX · THE WITNESS OF POVERTY

AS ORIGINAL sin touched all of creation, so too has the Incarnation of our Lord given new meaning and reality to the world of material things. In the Church there has always been a tension between these perspectives, between the world we are in and the following of our Lord according to the counsel of poverty.

All these tensions will not be resolved easily. The problem we are dealing with is one that has not yet received a final, full, adequate, theoretical solution. There are still different points of view. There are different emphases, different spiritualities of poverty; and even today there are different theoretical understandings of poverty. These will not be reconciled soon. This fact should not disturb us unduly because we have the guidance of the Church. If the Church approves or tolerates certain forms of poverty today, we can peaceably accept those forms.

Poverty is certainly one of the essential traits of New Testament spirituality. One may wonder precisely why that should be. If we could start our considerations at a very basic level, we might ask why material goods or the deprivation or abstention or juridical use of them should be considered a special trait of New Testament spirituality. What is there so important about poverty? Is it not a kind of inverted materialism to think that deprivation of material goods is in any way a path to evangelical spirituality? There are many higher goods in the order of values. Could it not be said that deprivation of honor, or deprivation of power, or deprivation of love would be a far more efficient means for uniting ourselves with God? And if we consider poverty purely from the aspect of asceticism, this might be so.

There is about poverty a kind of mystery. The Old Testament placed the poor in a very special situation. To a certain extent, today, with the advancement of a technological situation and with an affluent society, we have lost touch with what might be called the sacramental aspect of poverty or the essence of poverty as a Christian mystery.

In New Testament spirituality, evangelical poverty preceded that which has become, in our modern day, the archetypal virtue of the religious, obedience. The early ascetics gathered together in the desert to lead a common life characterized by poverty. This poverty was later submitted to obedience. The abbot or ruler of the poor community was a spiritual director or spiritual father for the individual. Obedience was not so clearly formulated at that time as poverty was.

What was the original meaning of that poverty, and has poverty changed in its Christian and ascetical meaning since? This is a question which is not easy to answer. The primary objective or motivation of those who chose poverty in the primitive Church was an assimilation to Christ crucified, Christ stripped and annihilated, a sense of what it meant to be rich in giving and in having nothing, and at the same time a freedom for the contemplative life. Does poverty provide that kind of freedom for prayer today?

An assimilation to Christ crucified, to the mystery of the cross, will be seen in Christian poverty throughout its history; but there will be various emphases on that motivation. A basic distinction might be marked between the Franciscan understanding of poverty and the Dominican. These are not opposed, but the Dominican understanding of poverty, which is more common today, relates poverty more closely to the efficiency of the apostolate. It is not reduced exclusively to a means for the apostolate, but that emphasis is strong. This is the form of poverty that has survived most predominantly in the contemporary Church. Today there is a movement which returns to the Franciscan idea of poverty, which emphasizes social assimilation to Christ's poor.

One of the earliest meanings given to poverty—and one that continues to our day—is that of eschatological witness. We, as poor Christians, must bear witness to the fact that we do not have here a lasting city, that our heart is not installed in this world. Our ultimate home, our *patria*, is not this world, and therefore we must use it as though we used it not. Seek first the Kingdom of God and then all these things, whatever is necessary for your human life, will be added to you. The first objective is the advance of the Kingdom of God. The poor man or poor woman stands as public witness within the city of man to the fact that this is not our final city. In this way, also by the poverty of virginity, the virgin stands in the same situation, pointing, within the Christian community, to the fact that our eternal homeland is not yet here. On the other hand, the last days of the Church have arrived. We are living in the ultimate period, between the coming of the Paraclete and the coming of the Parousia. In this tension between present-day existence and future existence, we are always pointing toward the future.

Another meaning attached to poverty is related to the basic affirmation of faith in the supernatural order and in Providence. God will care for our needs; there does exist an order of reality in which God intervenes in our human life, as He constantly intervened throughout salvation history. This, we know, has been the experience of the saints who have particularly loved poverty. They have emphasized this aspect of poverty more than any other: it is a rejection of exclusively natural means for obtaining things we stand in instant need of—food and shelter and those things which allow us to survive as human beings. It is a casting of our care exclusively upon the Lord whose ways are not our ways, but who is a living and protective Father and is aware that we have need of these things. Often, in the legends of saints, we observe this utter commitment of faith in the supernatural order: God is aware of our human situation with all its uncertainties and needs. We see the insistence of saints that nothing be left in the house, but that all that is left over when we have eaten sufficiently should be thrown out. We know the legend of the saint replying to his companion when the companion remarked that he personally had saved something from yesterday because he had today received no alms. "Get rid of that at once, and then you will receive alms."

There are many legends of the saints' providing supernaturally for the needs of their community, of their resolute determination not to be swayed by natural prudence from their adhesion to faith in the provident God. St. Theresa insisted, when it appeared contrary to all human prudence, that she would accept no moneys for her foundations, since their primary purpose was not poverty, but prayer. This was a question of considerable agony to her because she was eager to establish more houses. She was well aware of the scale of values involved. Yet she could not receive money for founded houses because it appeared to her that this would be a withdrawal from her first-chosen position: total faith in the existence of the supernatural order and the God who would provide for her needs.

Poverty is also, and has been throughout Christian history, a form of asceticism. It is rare, however, that we find the ultimate spiritual explanation of Christian values in the fact that they involve self-denial. So many forms of self-denial could be self-chosen that we have always to ask why poverty was singled out. The ultimate explanation of poverty is not that it denies man something he would quite naturally seek for. So also with virginity: the fact that it allows us to court an undivided heart and give up a great human good is not necessarily the ultimate value. This is one aspect of its value, but, normally, virginity has other aspects.

One additional, and under-emphasized, aspect of poverty is the specific aid that it is to humility. This is not always underscored by ascetical writers. Most of us are not so much attached to the sheer possession of money as we are attached to those things which money can buy and particularly to those things which flatter self-esteem. This is obvious to anyone who has lived in a world where money is plentiful. It is a curious thing, but if one, poorly dressed, drives up to a hotel or a restaurant, he gets a different reception than the richly dressed get. This happens in almost all human situations. The possession of money aids toward an assured position in the world. The non-possession of money is an important aid to humility, submission, acceptance of suffering, acceptance of an inferior position in this world.

Christian poverty is not, of course, a poverty that would deny the relative value of this world's goods. That kind of poverty would not be Christian because Christ, in His Incarnation, has prolonged Himself in the universe and has consecrated the universe and material goods to a destiny. The world, matter, goods, have a dignity and a value which we should not disregard. It is not out of contempt for mate-

rial goods, therefore, that we abstain from them. Sometimes
the writings of that great apostle of poverty, Leon Bloy,
intimate almost a radical horror for material goods. This
creates a certain uneasiness in one trained in the Christian
tradition.

The question raised so frequently today in any consideration of religious poverty is: does religious poverty establish
us in any solidarity with the genuinely dispossessed? Is this
its ultimate meaning in a Christian universe? There can be
no doubt that during certain periods of history, the position
of the dispossessed left the Christian, if he collaborated with
it, in a favorable spiritual position—if he freely chose or accepted it for Christ's sake. But is this the primary function of
poverty today? Has the world advanced so far in the welfare
state, with planned economy, that this function of poverty is
gone? In other words, would religious, by establishing a solidarity with the dispossessed of this world, be fulfilling the primary function of poverty? Or is it rather my obligation as a
Christian to work confidently toward that situation in which
there are no more dispossessed? I would then render myself
obsolete as a poor man. To a certain extent, this has been the
tradition, has it not, in the past, with Christians? They possessed genuine, not symbolic, solidarity with the dispossessed, but they also worked to bring to a higher level the
economic standards of those around them.

Poverty also insures a relative freedom from the solicita-
tions to pleasure and by so doing can bring men to maturity,
for the pleasure principle that governs the life of an infant
should not govern the life of an adult. Money is not simply a
symbol of something. It also has the capacity to produce. It
has the capacity to produce a certain freedom from the
thorns of life. It also has the capacity to produce for us

pleasure, and pleasure, while not wrong, has an immanent tendency to invade the whole of life. The individual who becomes more and more devoted to pleasures gradually tends to lose the depth of his life, humanly speaking, and also to be unable to reach the depths of the supernatural order. Pascal pointed this out in the seventeenth century. Pleasure-glut can be one of the sources of atheism, of the basic inability to confront and believe in the existence of an Infinite over me who is totally other than I.

One of the sources of atheism has been labeled *distractio*. We might question whether this is not becoming more and more a source of atheism. God has become an unnecessary hypothesis, to use the words of La Place. Our life is so cluttered with activities, so filled with *distractio*, so much drawn to peripheral activity that we are no longer able to concentrate on the great fundamental truths of man's situation with regard to the Infinite. We can no longer dispose of ourselves with regard to the Infinite as a result of the superficiality of our life. The man of *distractio* is sometimes not even able to commit great sins. The fact that money can produce pleasures can lead toward a gradual submission to the instinctive life of man. Where pleasure rules, a kind of immersion in matter takes place, which is incarnated in a way of life, a way of action, a way of dealing with others. This kind of absorption into the world of matter and pleasures, of the instinctual, may cause other values to dim. In a predominantly "fun culture," one has at times the impression that one is dealing with highly developed animals rather than with human beings. Intellectual and spiritual life can be so assimilated to the level of instinctual life, of immediate goals and immediate goods, that it becomes sub-human. Poverty militates against that style of life.

Another value of poverty is the freedom it gives from the attitude of the exclusively "business," and excessive concern with administration, management, development, and growth of possessions. We cannot place freedom from this type of preoccupation as an ultimate value since in any organized group there are going to be individuals whose life is going to be concerned with business, if the rest of the community are to eat.

The meaning of poverty simply cannot be a type of freedom from responsibility which would correspond to a spiritual infantilism. Poverty fosters that kind of childlikeness which is recommended in the Gospels, but not that infantilism where one is taken care of by others and freed from responsibility to choose. We need responsibility for material things, unless there is a higher responsibility committed to us, such as the apostolic life. Also life in a contemplative Order, of praying for the Kingdom of God, has direct and intimate responsibility. The fact of being freed from responsibility for material possessions could not possibly be the ultimate meaning of Christian poverty.

Recent studies have also criticized the sociological idea of poverty. We should not identify religious poverty, poverty for the sake of the Kingdom of God, with assimilation to the lowest paid workers. Rather than identifying ourselves with the lowest in the wage-scale, we should reflect upon our Christian obligation to bring about those material, social, political, economic conditions in which that group will be elevated. I personally wonder whether one can do this unless he has some kind of empathy with that group. If he does not have a type of identification with the lowest paid, will his concern for their elevation really touch anything at the depth of his existence? Will it not be the kind of easy acceptance of certain expressions of the Gospel, such as "the poor we will always have with us"? Christ did not say that by our activities we should arrange that the poor will always be with us.

As we live poverty today in the religious life, we are hardly identifying with the lowest elements in the economic scale. Certainly, evangelical poverty does not have to be identified with destitution. Christ had what he needed to live by. After all our meditations on the poverty of Christ in the cave, we have to admit the cave was more comfortable than the inn where He would have been otherwise. Joseph, at the time when Christ was born, was probably well paid. At the same time, it is evident that there is a problem area here. "In what sense are religious really poor?" Do religious share that kind of basic insecurity which characterizes the poor? To what degree should we be assimilated to the life of the economically poor? To what degree are we assimilated? Is there, besides the *de facto* problem of material goods, a spiritual and symbolical significance to them which alters their meaning as purely material goods? Over and over again, I have heard all over the world individual religious who express great distress that their food was so good. In relationship to the country in which they lived and the working class with which they lived, it was good. I suggest that possibly we should not consider these elements in too devaluized, unrelated, materialistic a fashion. We should not necessarily be critical of religious groups which provide dinners the poor would not be able to provide. Perhaps these meals have a more sacramental, symbolic significance: that we are here to rejoice, that we are here to relax.

There are also psychological conditions to be considered. When one feeds 300 at one serving, it is likely that the results will be different, both psychologically and materially, than if one fed three. To prepare mussels for 300 might probably mean inedible mussels; it might be true that, in a poor family, this might be a delicacy and, in its own way, less poor than the celebration meal occasionally set before a religious community. One must consider the tensions involved in a community of 300, or 200, or 20, or 10, five of whom are actively opposed to me, seven of whom passively opposed, two of whom are not aware that I am in the community yet, and so forth. The common meal can have different significance from a family meal and perhaps should be somewhat better than the food of the poor.

Theologians today insist also that it is not the common sharing of goods which constitutes the religious meaning of religious poverty! Let us suppose, for example, that ten millionaires decided to share all their goods in common for religious motives. Would this be in any sense genuine poverty? If the sharing of goods in common is only a means, to what end is it a means? Is it a means to the apostolate? This would be more or less the Dominican-Ignatian point of view. Or is it a means to the dispossession of one's self, as the Franciscans would hold? Is collectivism the only solution? There is a kind of collectivism which is in apparent opposition to capitalism. Is it a real solution? In certain religious communities, is not the amount of material goods held and the quality and general style of life of this group so elevated that one could say that poverty must have altered its meaning, if these religious are to be called poor? Private property is not condemned by the Church. Collectivism simply for *collectivism's* sake is not the ultimate meaning of Christian poverty.

Some theologians believe that religious poverty really should not be defined with regard to goods, but with regard to God. That is a valid insight, but what does it ultimately mean? The genuinely poor man is the faithful man, the trustful man, the man who is constantly open to the suggestions of the Holy Spirit and who wishes to structure his life theonomically. He structures his entire approach to reality, to persons, to situations, by the will of God intimated to him in the concrete circumstance of his situation. The poor man is then automatically put in opposition to those who oppose God, by power, by status, by position, by riches. Poverty implies an openness to risk. It seems to some that the deprivation of material goods or the use of material goods within a framework juridically approved by the Church is really not in any sense an *evangelical* value. It may be a preparation for something else. It could be a training to adjust to a situation where we would be called to fulfill the will of God under difficulty. It could be an exercise to prepare us for that situation when we will be called upon to fulfill the will of God in a situation which we would not ordinarily call poverty, but which demands an awareness and readiness to accept His will in suffering, difficulty, frustration, in denial of that which is perhaps most close to our egotism. It would involve an unprotected situation in the world.

There is a very beautiful text of Chrysostom in which he comments on Christ's words "And I send you as a lamb among wolves." Chrysostom insists that if one is going to arm himself as a wolf, the Lord doesn't say He will protect him. It is the unarmed one, the defenseless one, whom the Lord says He will bless. One must stay as a lamb among wolves, not be a wolf among wolves, or a more powerfully-armored wolf among wolves, because then one has no guarantee of divine protection. It is only the one who is defenseless whom He will protect. Poverty is a kind of discipline, as silence is a discipline, to prepare for recollection and prayer. Silence in itself is not an absolute; it does not have evangelical value, but it is something which creates a condition for the free expansion of prayer, of active and affective recollection. So poverty would be an unprotected situation in the world which would open us to the possibility of hearing the invitation of the will of God, in a situation where He called on us to surrender things. Poverty might be much less a poverty of material things, in its ultimate, spiritual meaning, than a poverty of influence. It would foster the humble situation in the world, where one's influence was altered or destroyed or attacked. There is a poverty of reputation where one is not well thought of, considered a fool—as Christ was —and wears the livery of Christ. There is a poverty of power where one is not in a situation to say, as the centurion in the Gospel, "I say this and it is done." Rather, poverty of situation would imply: "I say this, and no one pays any attention. I am inept and defenseless and I am powerless." This notion of poverty has a deep spiritual significance, yet this attitude is covered in Christian tradition under other virtues rather than under the virtue of poverty itself, which has always been understood in direct relationship to material goods.

The substitution of God's aim for my aims is certainly a Christian desire. Poverty of self-will is certainly a Christian desire, if it has not been a classic understanding of the vow of poverty. Karl Rahner has other contributions to give to this uncertain understanding of poverty. As usual, Rahner's contributions lie first in clarifying what a thing is not. Rahner comments that poverty is not simply dependence. Juridical dependence on the will of the Superior does not mean poverty; and if we insist upon considering it as such, we will simply evolve into a situation in which we could be rich and yet follow the vow of poverty. Moreover, if we take dependence as our ultimate norm, we could juridically deviate from the law in its ultimate function and purpose to achieve a solution which, at the same time, maintains the letter of the law and destroys its spirit. And if the style of the particular monastery in which I live is so rich that I live in the style of a man who has a hundred thousand dollars a year income, one ought to question whether I am really poor. A very rich medieval abbey—and in saying *medieval*, Father Rahner is very kind, for I am sure his experience is more direct and modern—a very wealthy medieval abbey, even if the monks were perfect in absolute dependence in regard to the Superior, would not constitute a favorable situation for evangelical poverty. If a situation arose in which I could have a Lincoln Continental, could have yearly trips around the world which cost twenty thousand dollars, with permission, something would have gone wrong, not with the legal formulation extant in this particular constitution, but in the adjustments of this series of laws to the charismatic insight of the founder. Poverty varies, of course, from Order to Order. The poverty of the Cistercian need not be the same poverty as the Franciscan or the Jesuit. St. Dominic pointed out, on the occasion when the Cistercians went to convert the Cathari, that they would have done better if they had left their legion of noble horses at home. The Cathari despised material things; and when they saw the wealthy Cistercians bounding in, they were not likely to return to the poor Church of the poor Christ.

There is, however, a legitimate scale of variation in styles of living. There is a scale of variation between country and country. One noted religious Superior was deceived when he instructed a group of religious men to fix their poverty ac-

cording to the scale of living of the secular priest in the
country in which they lived. In some countries, the secular
priests live quite well. The adjustment upward was rapidly
made!

Religious poverty must be adaptable to the apostolate of
the group. And yet if a particular apostolate requires a style
of living which is really characteristic of the rich, should not
this apostolate be carried on, not by religious who are dedicated to evangelical poverty, but rather by the laity? Here
one must distinguish. The distinction between corporate and
private possessions is common. We cannot, however, accept
it with unqualified approval or apply it in all cases equally.
"I personally do not possess all the things." But in the real
order, do I not? There are very few religious who would
appropriate another's belongings, clothes, car, office, TV. It
would be a rare religious who would borrow possessions
which are the possessions of the community, and not an individual's. In practice, have such possessions not become
regarded as "my own"? We must adapt poverty to the apostolate—but how far can we adapt and really keep the meaning of evangelical poverty?

Some theologians insist that poverty must imply some real
deprivation of material goods. Unless one in some manner or
other feels the effect of poverty, in what sense can he be
called a poor man? But in the contemporary attacks upon
the notion of poverty based on "dependence," are not certain
points missed, namely, that one of the joys of being rich is
personal disposition of possessions? Even though I live
within a community which provides me with things which
would not be provided to the destitute, perhaps not to the
working class, perhaps not even to the higher working class,

still if it is not I, as a person, who decides what use shall be made of this money, I am, in some sense, poor.

Take, for example, the question of food. Perhaps the group in which a religious works feeds him very well. Perhaps because it knows what the normal American male likes, it feeds him steaks three times a week for breakfast and five times a week for dinner and the intervening lunches are prime ribs of beef, rare. Is this poverty? It still could be! Why? Because if he were in possession of his own money, a man might prefer and choose a Chateaubriand once a week and Dover sole the other days. Or perhaps he would like to have a splendid feast on Monday night and fast the rest of the week, as long as he had once a week the type of feast which he personally chose. There is a certain deprivation in dependence. Community dispositions of goods are not my free organization of what I possess as an extension of my personality, to express my personality. An independent man might like to live in a very poor section of town, but in his private room have the best art. Or perhaps he would like to live in a situation in which he simply enjoyed beauty, a beautiful view even if he were living in a shack. In poverty of dependence, he cannot choose these things; his freedom is limited as the freedom of the poor is limited. There is a certain poverty there. That poverty is not to be condemned. If the individual who accepts it is mature, he would normally have certain ideas on how he would use his money, and he cannot exercise them. It is true that mere collectivism or mere dependence does not make one genuinely poor. What, then, is it to be poor in the evangelical sense? What is the motive? The motive seems to have shifted somewhat in the course of centuries. Imitation of Jesus Christ, or the assimilation to Jesus Christ crucified, is a motive. Jesus Christ recommended poverty, but He did not recommend it specifically for communities.

Is poverty valuable because it makes the apostolate more effective? It does make the apostolate more effective, for without it I cannot easily reveal myself as a witness to the eschatological reality of faith. If I cannot come to humanity committed to the cross in the Christian life, my apostolate is not going to be effective, no matter how skillful I am. But this was not necessarily the motive of the early ascetics who chose poverty.

Is it a kind of mystical identification with Christ? I think we have to reflect much more on this question.

Is it simply an organizational device for corporate efficiency? If we keep all this money in common, can we make a more effective use of it? I do not think this was the original meaning of poverty. We have to consider a great many problems in the concrete. In what sense can we witness to the eschatological reality if we live in a twelve million dollar building? On the other hand, we have an apostolate that requires this. In America, there may be no "scandal" whatsoever connected with this. There may be a modest scale of living within that building which doesn't disturb anyone. Certain Christians today, however, are disturbed by such religious buildings. If the Church has a need for this type of apostolate and the apostolate needs this type of building, it seems reasonable to use it. Poverty also allows the use of offices, machines, cars, trips, leisure, contemplation of beauty. Poverty should not deprive us of beauty. No matter how simply our situation is, we need something that raises our minds to the contemplation of the Lord by way of beauty. A chapel may be very poor, but it need not be something that makes one nauseous.

The eschatological witness so prominently recalled by spiritual authors also reminds us that poverty removes great obstacles to perfection, namely, the obstacle of power and the obstacle of pleasure and, to a lesser extent, the obstacle of security. Have we grown lax with regard to poverty? If by poverty we mean the visible, incarnational representation of man's fundamentally insecure position before God in this world, of His fundamental contingency, then it would seem that many would have to answer: we have grown lax. We really do not experience any fundamental economic insecurity. Barring unexpected persecution, most religious today know that they are going to have enough to eat as long as they live. They know that they are going to have a room of some sort, howsoever small or large, and they are going to have excellent medical care and a solid education. Their old age is going to be taken care of. This presents a valid difficulty. To a certain extent, instead of witnessing to the insecurity of man's situation in the world before God and testifying to Divine Providence, many in the modern world see us as a kind of glorified trade union. We have all the fringe benefits so that we will be assured of security all our life, and so we are the least economically insecure of people. If, therefore, poverty's radical meaning is that kind of insecurity, then it seems that to a certain extent we have grown lax.

Secondly, is the religious style of life, of food, of rooms, of medical care, of travel, in any real sense, poor today? Could we, without exaggerated devotion to the past, return to a simpler style of existence? Or is this really not practical if we are to continue our apostolate effectively? If it is not possible and the Church wants and approves this apostolate for religious, or at least has not disapproved it, we should be able to go on with peace.

Has it come to the point where poverty in religious groups today is nothing but worldly wealth in common? Is poverty a genuine witness to solidarity with the poor? Is that needed as much as it once was, with a planned economy? Does witness to the solidarity of the dispossessed have the same influence that it always had? I suspect that it does.

Are we really poor or are we lax? We are rich in such things as foster the goals of our own particular group. Take such things as books. These are necessary. It does not mean that we are lax if we have all that is required for our work as a teacher. Should we define poverty theologically, as an asceticism in consumable goods and luxury? We should restrict ourselves with regard to consumable goods and certainly with regard to luxury goods. There should be, secondly, a community of goods and a *common* way of life *for all*. That common way of life should serve to some extent as a witness to a readiness to self-denial, to participation in the mystery of the cross, to openness to charity. We should always be open to give to others and be concerned with others who have less than we, and poverty should witness to our own contingency before God, to our advent situation, waiting for His grace.

The values of religious poverty are witness values— witness to faith in the supernatural order, witness to hope in a future world and in the Providence of God over life in this world. It is not I who must provide against every possible contingency, but the Lord of history will provide in every concrete situation. Above all, poverty should witness to solidarity in love with men, with humanity as a whole. It implies freedom also—freedom from attachment to power and security and pleasure, to wealth, to the things wealth brings us, freedom for the apostolate so that we do not have to actively engage in business in order to pursue our apostolate.

Another value of religious poverty that is not underscored sufficiently is this: poverty is a kind of reconsecration of the created world to Christ, reconsecration either by contemplation or by detachment from the world. Sometimes those who do not possess can contemplate more fully than those who do possess. This kind of reconsecration of goods would put them back into the hands of Christ. In so doing, the religious imposes a spiritual destination on a created, material thing; this furthers the redemption of matter when matter was taken up into the divinity at the Incarnation and the Redemption.

Religious poverty is also an affirmation of hope. We expect all from the living Christ and not from our own ingenuity and our own ability. We have a certain freedom in that things no longer possess us. We stand in a relationship of complete detachment. They do not own us and therefore we are able perhaps to appreciate their ultimate reality and meaningfulness better than if we did possess them and had to worry about their continued possession and increase. This witness to detachment and freedom may be beneficial not only to the rich but also to the poor.

Poverty has a relationship to faith, to hope, and to love. With regard to poverty's relationship to faith, we must stress that it requires some genuine deprivation, not a purely juridical one. Unless we bear witness to the eschatological reality, our Christian poverty has lost its meaning. It may still be a very valid style of life in the Church, but it would not necessarily be evangelical. In its relationship to hope, poverty implies that we must leave the natural bases of our security and launch out into the deep. This is concretized and rendered visible to the world in that we do not possess that kind of security which man naturally strives for. This is possible even in an organization possessing large means. Poverty should have a sacramental visibility to the external world.

Poverty has a relationship to love. We should recall that the works of love, of compassion, of mercy in which Christ was most conspicuous have been done in the Church by those who have been genuinely poor. That orphans had mothers and fathers, more often than not, was due to the voluntarily poor. Orphanages and hospitals and schools were conducted by those who had chosen this way of poverty. To minister to the poor in works of love has been characteristic of poor religious.

Poverty also requires common life. In this area lies one of the real crises of evangelical and religious poverty today. In fact, one might question whether or not the poverty of common life, which is canonically one of the bases of religious life, genuinely exists today. Does common life genuinely exist in various houses of the same Order, or even within the same house? It is curious to note the wide scale of differences in the style of life lived within one religious family from house to house. In certain male religious houses, the religious are given a certain amount of money, commonly called travel money. This is used for various businesses not directly connected with the apostolate of the group, to tip the barber, for instance. To have all these minutiae regulated to the last detail is more complicated with the feminine temperament or at least is more easily tolerated by them. A certain amount of money is often given male religious; in some communities, each week to those who ask for it. It is not salary. But curious divergences in scale exist. One group of the same religious family, in the same town, the same country, in this particular house may get five dollars a month. Another house of that same family, with the same apostolate, same work, same education, will get fifty dollars a month. The scale is different, and it is rather an ample range of difference—ten to one. Is there a kind of hidden chicanery here? The common assumption may also be that one restricts himself to five dollars a month or fifty dollars a month. It is only a symbol of the Order's generosity and devotion to each individual. If it were an operative symbol of chicanery, such a custom might involve a tacit permission to use anything one can lay hands on, and this would certainly be contrary to the spirit of common life.

Religious often note certain divergencies in regard to health care. If, for example, the ordinary religious gets a cold, he goes to work or he goes to bed. He does not go to Florida or Caracas or wherever the healing sunshine happens to be at the moment. Superiors often do. These differences exist. It is true that the apostolate of some within the community is more externally valuable than that of others. One may be a teacher; the other, an administrator. Overseeing many may require a certain degree of health not required of others. Still it would seem that this practice of discrimination should be indulged in with considerable reluctance both on the part of the one enjoying Caracas and on the part of the one giving permission to enjoy Caracas. Otherwise there might come a fundamental conviction that either colds are essentially different when they occur in a person of higher status, or there might occur a conviction that there are essential grades of religious.

There is also the question of those machines which are

necessary to implement and extend the apostolate. Judgment as to their need can vary in the course of time. There was a time when a fountain pen was considered a luxury. There was a time when a typewriter was considered a luxury. Now the question is rather whether one can have an electric typewriter and a secretary to run it. The differentiation of work within a group may require different instruments. It is possible that a religious in a certain position may require, not only a secretary, but a number of secretaries to carry on his work effectively. The inner spirit of poverty would urge that he see whether he can do without one or the other—or leave them, on those days when they are empty-handed or occupied only in doing their nails, to be employed by others.

In the area of travel, also, there are certain indications that common life may be suffering from a re-interpretation which implies a genuine danger. If it is necessary that a religious travel, he should travel in the way that befits a religious, with his particular apostolate. Some unreasonably criticize administrators because they have automobiles to carry them where they have to go. This can be unreasonable. The expenditure of time and energy, if they didn't have cars, would reduce efficiency. Such inefficiency would not be the spirit of a group which requires that means be adapted to ends.

On the other hand, most automobiles carry one with relatively equal efficiency to one's destination. A Ford, for example, generally speaking, will get one there just as rapidly as a Lincoln Continental. I once gave a series of conferences for five hundred women Superiors in the East, and it was astonishing to note the variety of equipment in which they arrived. Some on their feet—possibly they didn't have very far to go. Others were picked up by their friends. Others

arrived in chauffeur-driven Cadillacs, hired, I am sure, just
for the day. Others drove themselves. No one came on a
motorcycle or a motorbike. The whole gamut of means to
arrive at their destination seemed to be used there, from the
richest to the poorest. Perhaps the image given to those observing this procession might not give credit to a dedication
to evangelical poverty, especially if we indulge too exclusively in Lincolns and Chryslers and Cadillacs. These things
occur. Whether they are abuses or legitimate developments
of poverty ought to give us pause. So also on travel. We do
have to get to various places. There was a time when it was
considered against poverty to fly. Some have been told: "No,
you cannot come back by automobile, although it would
cost less, because you would see more and therefore you
must fly." There can be complicated questions as to what
precise virtue is at issue here. Is it obedience, in a dark,
obscure fashion, or genuine poverty that is at stake? Must
religious who have certain works or work, travel first class?
Traveling second class in Europe in order to be sure of a seat
may be reasonable. On a plane, one does not get in unless he
has a seat. The basic differences between first and second
class in the United States are trivial.

For those over six feet tall, first class provides someplace
to put their legs. However, a trip across this country is only
about five and a half hours from point to point, and this is
not too long to endure a moderate amount of discomfort. In
first class, one also enjoys unlimited quantities of champagne. If one feels that a particular facet of the apostolate
requires unlimited champagne, one could indulge in it in
economy class at one's own cost and save the great difference between first and economy. Almost any normal person's
consumption of champagne would be paid for many times

over by the difference. The third difference is the fact that
first class is a status symbol. This advantage would appear
less easily reconciled with the commitment to evangelical
poverty.

The custom of vacations is also becoming more widespread among religious orders. Some take vacations at the
house reserved for the community vacation; others take trips
around the world. There would be no objection to this if the
person genuinely needed such a vacation. A round-the-world
trip could be a substitution for expensive therapy if he or she
were on the verge of a nervous breakdown. If such a vacation were to avoid the expense of therapy, and return this
religious to calm and greater commitment to poverty and the
apostolate, few would object to it. But if it should become
sort of a common assumption that if one has a certain function within the group, he automatically gets a round-the-
world tour at regular intervals, we should re-evaluate the
connection between the function and poverty.

The function of an office, particularly the higher offices in
a religious administration, should represent something of the
evangelical spirit and the values for which this particular
group was founded. Within this whole realm of common life,
there is a large question as to how far a Superior should go
in indulging what is called extra- or praeter-legal ways of
obtaining things, whether they be a trip around the world or
a vacation here or a private home or a villa on Lake Como or
a private car. Permissions like these could lead to such a
confusion of obligation that poverty would no longer be
recognized. If a particular community has a tacit understanding with the administrator that anyone who could get a
private car may have a private car, one can imagine what
would happen. Those who came from rich families would

have Cadillacs, and those who came from poor families would have nothing. This would certainly create within the community a certain discontent. Is this possible? It is actual and frequent. It is also actual in regard to other things. I can recall being told by my provincial when I asked for a tape recorder to write a book, "Well, you may have the tape recorder, if you can get a gift of one." I find that a fascinating interpretation of poverty. If extended to a general principle, I can have both a Lincoln Continental and a tape recorder and a secretary tomorrow. As long as I live, I shall never want for any luxury. A principle should be universal. If I need a tape recorder for my work, I should have it. If one says, "Buy it out of your own money," then everything I can buy out of my "own" money is mine.

Different styles of life can arise within the same Order and within the same community. And these can cause pain and painful comparisons. Some of them would be extremely difficult to justify.

We have also to face the fact of economy. If a new house is founded that is *de facto* very poor and another house is founded that is rich, there are likely to be contrasts. We should try to keep these contrasts at a minimum. Within the same house, contrasts should be at a minimum. If I come from a wealthy family, this should not mean that my style of life within a religious community is different from others in that group. Yet this happens. The avoidance of privation can become a kind of private apostolate. Some seek out the richest in the social group because they press upon us vacations, spending-money, membership in exclusive golf-clubs, while others in the community have none of these advantages. Such a variation in style of life, if it were permitted to go unchallenged, could result in the destruction of the entire spirit of common life. The spirit of poverty would be destroyed. If I have friends who belong to eight different country clubs and all eight have told me to sign my name at least once a week, this gives me at least seven dinners and one lunch in a style to which I should not legitimately become accustomed. This occurs. It will require a certain re-thinking of objectives to eliminate what may become an abuse on so flagrant a scale as to destroy any validity to common life and produce a widespread cynicism.

Another problem of poverty and economy is difficult to solve because many of those who have loved the poor in the past have insisted that poverty does not mean economy. For example, St. Francis insisted that even though stones were less expensive, he wanted his hut built of wood because wood was more perishable. In one case, a magnificent estate was given to religious. The Superior insisted, at the cost of about two million dollars, upon stripping the building of its beautiful but luxurious equipment. I think St. Francis would have agreed with him.

So there can be a contrast between poverty and economy. Is it more in accord with poverty to buy three cheap suits which will wear out in three years or one good suit which would last ten years? One may make a substantial saving by buying the expensive. Which is more in accord with poverty? We should not, however, be so concerned with economy that we deprive religious of necessities. At times this occurs. In some countries there is an extreme mystique of poverty or economy. One continues to pile up money in the bank at the expense of the group which lacks sufficient food. I have lived in houses where a large percentage had TB because of malnutrition. They belonged to a wealthy province. There, economy had been overemphasized to the detriment of poverty. Poverty is also not penury; there should be a minimal sufficiency for the ordinary needs of ordinary men and women. One should not be expected to live on the kind of turnip that the Belgians call "standing water." Care should be taken for the individual to enable him to work. Even the Carmelites have to face this today. The generation of vocations they are receiving today are not quite so robust, temperamentally or physically, as they once were. There may be needed some adjustments in the amount and quality of food to enable them to do what they are supposed to do.

QUESTION. "Constitutions allowing religious women to live as mendicants are not common in this country. Active congregations have means of support which are reasonably adequate. However, many religious women continue to beg from their families, relatives, friends, business people. They do this for themselves personally and for their congregations, and some Superiors encourage it. Is this poverty?"

·ANSWER. A Superior should be highly reluctant to encourage this kind of benevolence unless they proclaim it openly to the community—and then divide the proceeds with the community. We have all known religious communities where Superiors would say, "We are very poor at the moment. Couldn't you get your own clothes from home?" The quality of clothes that come in will differ very much, then. This does not encourage poverty or common life. The underlying, unspoken rationalization for this practice is this: it is not contrary to religious poverty to have the latest in all kinds of gadgets and services, provided the regular income of the congregation is not diminished.

QUESTION. "In justice to the donors, should we not use money gifts as specified."

ANSWER. Yes! Sometimes religious groups do not use money for the purposes for which it was given. This can be another form of stealing. We might presume, in some cases, that the donor would be willing to see it used in any way the religious group wanted. In other cases, this is impossible. I think it is a scandal if we are continually going outside the ordinary framework of our religious poverty to ask our family and our friends to give us typewriters, and so forth. If we need these, we ought to have them provided. If not, there ought to be a general appeal made on the part of the congregation or the house, and we could list our family among those they can appeal to.

QUESTION. "Can you see any possibility for dialogue or maturity for the following group?

"At a retreat given to a group of religious, the retreat master stressed that under no circumstances were the religious to accept any of the recent teaching on the meaning and spirit of obedience."

ANSWER. That retreat master would do well to study his theology. Ascetical theology is a difficult discipline.

QUESTION. "The retreat master insisted that one must submit his intellectual understanding to the decision of the Superior, no matter what that decision. He also pointed out that the subject must give total and loyal support to all the decisions of the Superior, even if those decisions are erroneous."

ANSWER. Obedience of the intellect urges that one try to see the reasons that the Superior cannot reveal. He may see the larger whole which we cannot see. If the decision is clearly irrational, then the good Lord does not expect us to accept irrationality placidly. That is not the function of our intellect. Even if we tried to force it, the intellect will not assent. The only time the intellect can make a free assent is when there is no compelling, necessitating evidence. If there were necessitating evidence that the Superior were in error —if, for example, she took three million dollars to build a platinum flagpole—no one could give intellectual assent to this decision. Black and white cases are rare, however.

QUESTION. "When the retreat was over, the Superior made the following announcement: those who like the retreat master and agreed with what he had to say are free to discuss his ideas. Those who did not like him, keep silence."

ANSWER. If so, the Superior has no idea of religious life. She should not only be removed, but dismissed from religious life as unsuitable. If she actually said this, we have to realize that while she did so with the best intention in the world, she is utterly and inconceivably ignorant of religious life.

QUESTION. "What does one do?"

ANSWER. Observe a prudent silence in the public manifestation. Get her aside later and try to bring her closer to the world of reality. From the psychological point of view, it is possible that the picture indicates serious mental illness.

QUESTION. "How can a subject help a Superior who seems to have the problem of insecurity with regard to her authority?"

ANSWER. Encourage her. One difficulty is that Superiors

think that if subjects ask questions, this means they do not wish to obey. Not at all. There is normally a great willingness to obey and even to try to find rational justification for difficult commands. I do not think that Superiors always recognize that. At times there is manifest a kind of childish desire that all agree with their own ideas and a kind of vanity, even a "king-complex," which is directly opposed to all Christian insights.

QUESTION. "I seem to be familiar with your recommendations: 'Be kind, pray, and be still.'"

ANSWER. I do not always recommend keeping still. I recommend speaking out only to that degree where there is a prudent hope that, even if I suffer, some good will emerge for the group. If the sort of situation you describe is common in your Order, you ought seriously to ask whether a normal person could join or remain in that group. It may also be doubted whether God would invite any normal person to join that group. Perhaps what you describe is only an isolated Superior in an isolated instance.

QUESTION. "You stated that the early Christians esteemed poverty before obedience."

ANSWER. I didn't precisely state that they placed poverty before formal obedience in the hierarchy of values, but that, historically, poverty became common as a means to perfection before the kind of juridical obedience we have today. The early Superiors were more spiritual directors. One was free to consult them, to obey or not obey. We might reflect upon this. This was once the insight of the Church.

QUESTION. "Is obedience emphasized because the primal instinct in man is for self-preservation, and the religious wish to empty themselves to follow Christ?"

ANSWER. Yes. However, at a certain state of development, there are other powerful instincts in man. In mature individuals, personal integrity and liberty are of higher value than possessions and more difficult to abdicate than material possessions. Material possessions are often employed simply as a means of shoring up freedom and independence.

QUESTION. "I have heard it said that when a religious leaves the congregation, the fellow religious he leaves behind should examine their consciences. Please comment on this."

ANSWER. When we see many defections, we ought seriously to ask whether we have contributed in any way to a person's inability to find God in religious life. If we create a notion of obedience such that it is impossible for a free adult to obey, then we will spawn our own apostates from the group. We can sit back piously and say, "Oh, it is obvious he never had the spirit of obedience." The Pharisees placed intolerable burdens on others and did not lift a finger to bear them themselves. There should be a kind of corporate responsibility for the happiness of the individual; yet, on the other hand, we know that certain personalities can have difficulties which make their continuance in a religious group impossible. The Church admits this when she releases them from vows. We do not always know the reasons why people leave. We could and should examine our consciences as to what the concrete, social situation was in our group. In the concrete, social situation, was there ever any manifestation of genuine acceptance, or affection, love, desire to help, appreciation for the work she was doing for the community, for her ability to live as a human being?

QUESTION. "Your remarks relative to conditions in a religious house as being an occasion for developing a neurotic symptom in Sisters prompts this question. Laboratory experimentation indicates that individuals placed in impoverished and erratic environment tend to become disoriented with neurotic and psychotic tendencies. Psychologists use the term 'brainwashing' and 'mental manipulation' to designate the techniques to produce these states of mind. In some, not a few, novitiates, convents, conditions strongly resemble those created in laboratories for this kind of experiment."

ANSWER. A very interesting observation indeed. True.

QUESTION. "For example, Superiors decide which television program and radio program shall be allowed, and they themselves pontificate."

ANSWER. It seems obvious that if one is dealing with a group of adults, one should consult their preferences.

QUESTION. "All personal correspondence of the Sisters is rigorously censored."

ANSWER. That is probably just plain nosiness. When religious are adult, they should be able to write to whom they please without censorship.

QUESTION. "Assigned readings in college classes are passed on without regard to morality."

ANSWER. It is very difficult to make a moral judgment on

literature. It is a rare Superior who can make such a judgment since it demands specialization, which Superiors rarely possess.

QUESTION. "Reporting is encouraged."

ANSWER. I presume you mean tattle-taling—a disgusting habit!

QUESTION. "Even telephone conversations have to be reported in detail."

ANSWER. Such conditions are neurotic.

QUESTION. "Are not such conditions responsible for many almost-empty novitiates?"

ANSWER. Where they obtain, I hope the novitiate is empty. If those conditions exist, let us change them.

☷ SEVEN · MENTAL HEALTH IN RELIGIOUS LIFE

SEVEN YEARS ago, or even five years ago, almost no one would have considered this an important topic: today everyone who is able to read is aware that there exists grave concern about the psychological effects of religious life. What does religious life contribute to psychological maturity or to psychological immaturity? When we see religious houses in which twenty or thirty religious need psychiatric care, even the dullest can see there is a problem. Is the problem greater than in the past, or is it simply better recognized? It appears that it is greater than in the past and will continue to get even greater, until religious adopt the principle of mental health.

Even more profound a problem than that of mental breakdown is this: why are there so many "zombies" among the religious in religious life, those who function at a distressingly low level of mental efficiency? Why do so many religious live a "sheol" life as in the underworld of the hell of the Old Testament? In sheol, one was not precisely dead, but not precisely living either; one lived a dim, shadowy existence reduced to almost nothing.

Why is there so great a proportion of religious who live what we may call a plateau existence, able to cope with a certain minimal number of tasks a day, but beyond that capable of nothing—the type of persons who would be dishwashers in the world? Why are so many leaving? Many nuns who leave claim they leave because they fear they will end up total neurotics if they do not. As evidence for this they adduce the rest of their community—and this is not a very pleasant thought. Is the religious life in itself passé? There is nothing intrinsically wrong with this opinion. It could be that religious life once served the Church admirably, but is no longer necessary. Secular institutes could now take its place. This is not my conviction. But there are those who say that the factors which cause mental breakdowns are intrinsic to religious life. This seems impossible: after all, the Church has often confirmed religious life over the centuries. However, if a particular institute, as lived in the concrete, consistently produces neurotics, that institute will go out of existence. It not only will go out of existence, it is the absolute unconditioned will of God that it go out of existence. The Church may have confirmed a particular institute, but if the institute, as it is lived concretely, betrays the fundamental insights of the person who founded the institute, it will and should die.

There is a serious responsibility upon Superiors to dismiss neurotics and psychotics before they damage other personalities. Often such religious do eventually leave, but not before they can have damaged an entire community or a whole year or a whole generation of school children. One distinguished religious remarked, "In my personal formation of fourteen years I have never encountered a normal religious as a teacher." Neurotics can do incalculable damage in the classroom. Even more damage can be done if one of these unbalanced people gets into ecclesiastical power. Their neurotic judgment is then reflected not only in decisions concerning their personal lives, but in decisions which affect the lives of a whole generation of nuns or of priests or of Brothers or of schoolchildren.

Let us suppose a mythical individual who had what is jokingly called an "edifice complex." He wanted to build a great monument to himself and so spent twelve million dollars on a building which was clearly unnecessary. This is not only a twelve million dollar mistake, but other people have to pay for it, over a generation.

There are today great numbers of religious who are leaving upon recommendation of psychiatrists and their Superiors. However we cannot forget that they do not leave the first day that they become neurotic. In the interim they are centers of influence which poison the group in which they live.

The correlation between the specific training of the religious and mental disturbance or breakdown is the decisive point at issue. This is the question we must ask: are these factors something intrinsic to religious life? No, obviously, or the Church would not have confirmed the institute. But are they something produced by the concrete existential way this institute has been living? That is the important question. We have few psychological studies on that—for obvious reasons. Many today find it curious that so peaceful a life as the religious life should produce so many neurotics. Moreover, it appears from available studies that religious in general are not a great deal more neurotic than laymen. But one of the reasons for this proportion in the statistics is that there are few syphilitics among religious.

Where conditions in an entire group are sick, there develops something like a collective neurosis. In Nazi Germany a neurosis spread throughout almost a whole nation. This occasionally happens in religious groups where no one can challenge anything because the whole group has been brainwashed into a neurotic mentality. The neurosis becomes col-

lective. We recall on one occasion being in a religious house
with two psychiatrists. One said, "Do you realize that in this
house one can see the optimum conditions for neurosis?" It
can happen that 70 percent or 80 percent in a religious
community are neurotic without becoming aware of it since
they do not have the outside contacts and challenges which
might awaken them to their strangeness. The Nazis did not
think themselves odd. Is it the nature of the religious life
that produces this estrangement from reality? No. The nature of religious life is such that it is difficult; it can cause
conflicts and problems, but we do have the grace of God;
and if we believe in the supernatural, we realize that it is not
the life itself which produces neurosis. As a matter of fact, in
many houses it does not. In other Orders and institutions
and in particular houses of the same Order, it does.

What are the conditions *before* entrance into religious life
which tend to produce neurotic religious? Religious must
honestly face the fact that they have been negligent at times
in the candidates they have admitted. Until recently religious used no psychiatric examinations whatsoever for candidates. They simply admitted every pleasant type who
appeared on the doorstep, was healthy, appeared to want to
do the work which needed to be done, was willing to enter,
and showed some signs of virtue. Today we do have psychiatric examinations, which are still however very imperfect.
Today those who enter religious life come from a completely
different culture and background then that of 30, 40, 60, 90
years ago. Today's boy or girl often comes from a disturbed
home. In one seminary, out of 150 candidates for the priesthood 75 came from disturbed homes. This presents a problem immediately. A disturbed home produces, generally
speaking, a disturbed child. Moreover, today's world is expe-

riencing an intense shaking of all tradition. As a result people do not have the certitudes they once possessed. There is a cultural breakdown in the West which is obvious to sociologists and psychologists. Whenever a cultural breakdown occurs, one has psychological problems; the suicide rate goes up. Many of the candidates for religious life today come from homes where both parents worked. They have also had the experience of a continuing world war. They experience also the challenge to the whole economic structure of the West. Whether capitalism is moral or not disturbs young people. Western religious are also undergoing a considerable transformation. We are living in the age of the death of God in all its senses. There are sudden changes in ritual and dogma which disturb people, young and old. This is not an age of security, yet people need security for psychological maturity.

There is also visible a great shaking of tradition within theology. One observes the "instant theologians" as well as instant coffee. Some tell us that original sin is only a myth. They discovered this after one hour of study. Some tell us that Mary is not a virgin. She could not be a virgin for the simple reason that human love is great, and some cannot see any possibility of reconciling human love with virginity. There is also a crisis of obedience and authority. This crisis has spread to all those who come to religious life today. Young people can say, and mature theologians can say, in public and in private and in print, "I couldn't care less what the Pope says." This is indicative of an ambiguous understanding of authority. There is also great failure today to distinguish between authentic tradition and pseudo-tradition. For example, a nun may say, "It is traditional that we have the tassel hanging off this side, not off that side."

Possibly, if she examined tradition, she would find there were no tassels at all to begin with.

The tests that religious use today for candidates show up psychological problems, but they do not evaluate character and motivation. Character and motivation are nonetheless extremely important. A candidate who has a psychological problem, is aware of it, and has inner toughness, is a better candidate than someone who has that problem to a lesser extent, but has a flexible, gentle, mildly schizoid character. Unfortunately, in the past, many religious groups have preferred the type psychiatrists call schizoid, that is, the type which withdraws from reality, is very docile, malleable, formable, and likes to be given constant direction and orders. One may find that after a few years of religious life these become more schizoid and simply retreat into practical immobility, if not physical immobility.

Religious Orders have also fallen into the error of accepting candidates who are too young. Candidates should not be accepted before age 23 or 24. The answer often given to this idea betrays much: "We wouldn't get any vocations." In other words, "We can only expect the immature; an adult would never enter our group." It is better to do what is done in certain European countries, i.e., send candidates to a college or university and keep them in contact with the master or mistress of novices, once every two weeks, once every month. One should not accept candidates until they are grown-up. Religious should also examine carefully, *in depth*, into candidates' motivation for entering the religious life. Motivation will never be purely supernatural. Religious are human beings and hence are a mixture of the natural and the supernatural, the virtuous and the unvirtuous. A shrewd psychiatrist, however, in one lengthy interview could quickly spot certain fundamentals. Many people enter into the religious life with little supernatural motivation. Mothers, in certain cultural patterns, are enchanted that their son is to become a priest. He goes up in the social and economic scale. Moreover, he is unmarried; therefore, his wife will never interfere with mother. These vocations are artificially produced, but they are not infrequent, especially in certain ethnic groups. The author has witnessed two mothers of priests pulling hair because the son of one had been appointed to a position and the son of the other had not been appointed to that position. One would hope that the motivations of sons and mothers were not identical!

Some candidates are by temperament and background political religious. Being human, religious can be political. One meets nuns who have, by temperament, a desire for power. One meets careerists, who are willing to sacrifice anything as long as their career is advanced. For example, in one religious house, the seminarians had two reference books required for their work. Out of fifty students *one* had the use of them because they were stolen by that seminarian. This would have been a hint to a psychiatrist to recommend dismissal of that seminarian.

There are also those who enter religious life because of a fear of sexuality. This is more common than many realize. There are those today who believe that marriage is absolutely necessary for adulthood, for the personal maturity of every human being. The author is not of that opinion. However, many religious do enter religion because they have an unconscious fear of sexuality. No one is equipped to be a religious who is not equipped to be a good mother or a good father.

There is also a temptation to let in those energetic and

talented candidates who demonstrate a love of power. Power is one of the greatest motivation forces in human life. Sex is one, but power lasts longer. The desire for power can last forever. Religious should, therefore, be very careful in the selection of candidates. None should be admitted who fear responsibility or decision-making. Many schizoid types seek to enter religion precisely so that they never have to make a decision. Examiners should also be aware that some enter religion because of a spiritual sexual deviation—spiritual homosexuality or spiritual Lesbianism. This does not mean that they are practicing Lesbianism or homosexuality, but they are the type of person—seen not infrequently in religious life—who always have a chain of charming, open-minded, simple, sometimes good-looking boys or girls following them around. A grown-up would recognize the underlying current of psychosexual immaturity. Sometimes religious do not.

Granted that religious congregations admit all these types of personalities, as well as many normal people, what can they do with them after they enter? This raises the question of proper ascetical and psychological training.

It is, unhappily, quite customary to assign someone to train religious in the spiritual life who knows nothing whatsoever about it. No master or mistress of novices should be put to this work who does not have at least an M.A. in psychology, preferably clinical, and at least a year or two of training in ascetical theology. When masters or mistresses of novices do not possess an adequate formation, they train young religious by their own formation which is often already deformed by what they consider the "tradition" of their Order, their congregation, a tradition they have never had the opportunity to study historically. The result is often a spirit of legalism. When one really does not know anything, it is always safe to teach subjects to follow the "law." The law says your skirts should be one inch above the ground, and not two; therefore one concentrates on such pertinent, concrete details. This legalism is, of course, totally contrary to the evangelical principle of love and to the Gospel. It destroys people. It crushes individuality. Often, too, the master or mistress of novices feels that the safest course, since he or she does not know any spiritual theology, is to concentrate on what one might call "Christian moralism," that is, the theory that the moral virtues are the supreme virtues. For example, obedience is made the archetype of all Christian virtues. It is not, of course; charity is. One can discover this by reading the New Testament. Often little time is left for young religious to do that, for they are reading the rule book. This creates also an atmosphere of repression, of fear, of unwillingness to express personal individuality and of toadying to the master or mistress of novices. It is revolting to see adult religious a-flutter because their Superior, male or female, is arriving. Depending on the mood of "Father" or "Mother" today, the whole community reacts. This mentality is utterly childish, but it is often produced by the training given to religious. The training of masters and mistresses of novices often produces scruples. Sometimes those who train religious think that by producing a scrupulous conscience they are producing a sensitive conscience. Those masters and mistresses of novices who produce a scrupulous conscience are unwillingly producing an understratum of hatred and guarded hostility which can only reach up through the censor into consciousness in the form of scruples. But they do not know enough psychology to realize this.

The uninformed type of training described above produces at times a kind of intellectual gymnastics. The emphasis on authority and on obedience to "the mind" of the Superior produces a kind of mindlessness in the young religious; today my Superior is a democrat, and I am thoroughly democratic; tomorrow she is a monarchist, and I am a total monarchist. This is seen over and over again in religious life. Where is the adult independence of judgment? In its place is an infantile dependence, a clinging to this or that personality, the mistress of novices or the master of novices or the Superior, a childish regression to cradle life where one clings to the one mother or father figure available.

Religious should be aware of the fact that during the training period of young people, only men and women should be assigned to train them who are adult, who are trained, who are themselves open, warm, generous, mature, and human people. One must be a humanist to train human beings. Superiors should not be kept in office during those periods of life when men as well as women undergo unusual psychological stresses. Since in certain periods of life stresses become emphasized, one should not assign Superiors at those periods of life, e.g., the menopause, to train young religious.

Another disastrous factor in the early training of religious is isolation. One cannot help a person to be an adult in isolation from other men and women. Active religious should have no houses of formation in the country. Such houses should be in the city, and subjects should be in contact with human beings, and that includes "non-religious." When some religious returned from the War to their houses of formation, they noted that they had spent years in concentration camps, in exactly identical psychological conditions to those they experienced in their religious houses. This is serious. This isolation from reality can cause a real crisis of identity, Who am I? Religious have to be in contact with the stream of life. Novitiates and houses of study must move to the city. Candidates should go to the university, to Catholic universities, to non-Catholic universities. Religious could close most seminaries. There is no need for them. A priest could read theology under a theologian, while doing some work; when he knows enough theology, he can be ordained. Most houses of study are unnecessary. Nor can we approve of houses of formation where nuns take their juniorate, if they are a Charity nun, at a Charity college.

All too prevalent in the period of religious formation is an unconscious reliance on fear. No religious man or woman would deliberately create fear in another to force that person to do what is wanted, but one can do so unconsciously. A teacher can do it in the classroom. He can terrify students to force the students to do what he wants. So also religious Superiors can create an atmosphere of fear. We can recall one religious saying, "You know I've always been terrified of walking down that staircase because I was told it was reserved for the faculty."

The customary separation from the opposite sex is also a bad thing for the mental and religious formation of religious. To be normal a religious must have friends, including friends of the opposite sex. Religious should start their formation, *from the beginning,* in this situation. We look forward to the day when we will have many co-educational seminaries. They are already beginning. We will have many more of them. In Germany there is a movement which insists that there should be no seminary for men without at least some women in residence. It might teach the men some manners for one thing. They tend not to eat like animals when there are women around. The unfortunate fact is that in these isolated situations religious are being trained for a totally unreal life. They are being trained actually by deception, lies. For example, they are trained to a mode of spirituality concerning their life, let us say in a college or in a hospital, which is completely unreal. The first day they live in a college or hospital they discover that they simply cannot fulfill what their mistress or master of novices suggested or ordered. This causes conflict.

Religious must be on guard, too, against the homogenizing influence of the long black line. Perhaps someday, when we all wear different costumes, this influence will not be so effective. The reduction of individuals to a factor, or to a unit or to a number, cannot go on any longer. It was very successful in the past. It will not be successful in the present century. The only result possible is that religious will have nothing to reduce to uniformity because the present generation prizes its individuality. God Almighty, when He gives a vocation, prizes the individuality of this vocation. The reasons He gives an Order Joanna is not because she is Mary, but because she is Joanna. Some, by their training, do their best to make Joanna and Mary twins, psychologically. This cannot continue, and it will not continue because neither Mary or Joanna will remain. If a group wants to become extinct rapidly, it should homogenize its subjects. One can easily understand why people try to depress individuality. Individuals are much more difficult to handle than numbers or units. If one owns a herd of cows, he can get so much milk out of that herd, provided there is no influence which disturbs the herd. He can count on that, so much energy, so much productivity, or so much milk from the cows every year. If he has a group of individuals, they are much more difficult to handle. Nevertheless it is God who decided religious should be individuals, and not cows. Let us treat them as such.

There is also evident a great fear among religious of education. There were times in religious Orders and religious congregations when Superiors would not educate their nuns to an M.A. "Why," they said, "she will leave." This shows an extraordinary confidence both in the individual nun and in the group situation.

There are fears, too, created by adaptation which make for tension within the individual. Middle-aged people and older people, forced to adapt to situations they do not fully understand, and which have not been opened in dialogue with the community, will adapt, but there remains an inner conflict. This can cause many difficulties. There is also noted among today's religious a "conflict of rôles" which creates a psychological problem. "What am I to be? What is my identity? At one moment you ask me to be a child. I am not supposed to have any judgment. I am not supposed to make any decisions: you can do it all for me. You will tell me where to go, what subject to study, what to do, how to work, how to fill this file, everything. The next moment you want me to be a man. I am willing to be one or the other, but I cannot be both." This attitude manifests a conflict of role. The attempt to keep adults in a state of childhood results in neurotics or psychotics.

There is also a conflict of "professsional" rôle. "What am I supposed to be, a priest or a chemist?" This is becoming much more common today. "Why should I be a chemist if I am a priest?" "Why should I be a priest if I am a chemist?" "What should I do?" "What am I?" This is a conflict of "crisis of identity." We note also the crises that arise by the sudden shifts in the spiritual and intellectual wind. Sister Peter was Superior for six years: she insisted that the spiritual life was all important, studies and professional training, nothing. Six years I lived and fed on this, and tried to convince myself of it. Today she goes out of office and another enters, who says: "We do, by all means, need spiritual nuns, but first we have our work to do. How are you trained?" "Where am I? What am I?" This produces a conflict. The "conflict of ideal" is often between the ideal religious as presented by the mistress of novices or master of novices and what a man personally wants to be, as an individual, as a person, as what God made him. This can also cause a crisis of identity, which in turn fosters neurosis.

A frequent cause of neurosis is the pronounced lack of religious training for human affectivity. Many religious who have taken their final vows suddenly discover problems with human affectivity. Love is the center of the Christian life. It is the unique virtue; it is *the* virtue of the Christian life, and religious often fail to teach it in any way. They not only do not teach love: religious often seem to be afraid of loving. They do not seem to dare to love. They produce a stifled affectivity. A head is put on the geyser, but that geyser is going to burst somewhere. When it does burst, the personality is torn apart.

Religious usually fail to teach the nature of friendship. They give vague, mysterious warnings about "bad" friendships, "particular" friendships, without telling subjects what they mean by this, i.e., homosexuality. They often do not teach young religious what friendship is, and that religious life is a situation of friendship. In 1967, a worldwide organization of religious priests could gather together and could debate, for hours, whether friendship is possible to a religious! It is not only possible, it is a virtue, as one would see if he bothered to study the theology of friendship. Can religious become human and adult without friendship? They cannot. They will meet conflicts of all orders. They will experience conflicts in the sexual order. The author has encountered novitiates in which eighty percent of the novices were homosexual, overtly so. The fault lay, not with the innocent children who entered, but with the fiendish training that they received.

Religious rarely receive a realistic training on the nature of love and chastity. Their training is often negative, repressive, creating a fear of the other sex. Human beings need the other sex to be human. On the other hand there is a rebellion going on today. It is called "the third way." The "third way" recommends that religious hold hands, go to the beach together, she oils his back, he oils her back, and so forth. This is an expression of mutual esteem and affection. It is possibly harmless; but since men are composites natures, one should guard against the third way, which can produce frustration and tension.

"Without genuine oblative love, charity, religious life cannot exist," a noted psychiatrist said. It can exist, but it is not authentic religious life. It is the kind of neurotic existence that often substitutes for religious life. A Jesuit psychiatrist said that "the major problem in religious life, creating psychosis and neurosis, is affective immaturity." The author believes the major problem creating difficulties in religious life to be insecurity. The religious is brought up not to be personally secure. He or she is brought up to be dominated either by fear or by isolation, by lack of genuine, warm love around him or her, so that he or she is insecure. Out of this fundamental root of insecurity there springs venom, lack of charity, hatred, power-seeking. These vices are often an expression of sheer insecurity. The greatest thing religious could do to produce normal people would be give them a fundamental, radical, security—a sense that they are wanted in this group, loved, appreciated, not as a unit or as a factor, but as a concrete individual with all the faults, failings, limitations, and deficiencies which human beings have.

One of the greatest causes of immaturity and difficulty in the formational period is this lack of charity and support from the people with whom religious are living. One cannot easily have this if the community is more than twenty. One cannot actually have a religious community of more than twenty. It cannot exist. It is not a community. One may call it whatever one chooses, but it is not a community. Religious must break up houses, make them smaller. Moreover, one cannot have a province of one or two or three thousand religious. It cannot exist. One can pretend that is is a congregation, of course. A Mother Superior, Mother Provincial, Father Provincial has to know each subject personally and should visit each of them at least five times a year to discover their individual preferences, talents, tastes, development. When a religious of 30 years standing goes to meet his major Superior, and is greeted with the wrong name, things are awry. One can easily imagine how much confidence he has in making a "manifestation of conscience" to that Superior.

A major problem in the formation period of religious is boredom. Superiors often set people to do irrational work. Industry has found out that one of the greatest causes of neurosis is sheer boredom, routine. Religious need a change at regular intervals; they need different experiences, different people, different lectures, different opinions. One should not produce boredom and routine, and, especially, irrational unnecessary work: "Scrub this floor, already scrubbed twice; it will make you humble." It will not make the subject humble at all. It will just make him wonder why this irrational order was ever given, and if his group is given over to irrationality in general.

We note today a conflict which arises in the formation period from lack of communication. Do religious really talk to one another, really open up to one another, really know and love one another? Are they really a community of charity or simply a faceless, nameless group, a lonely crowd? We have heard the saying, "Religious enter as strangers, live together without knowing one another, and die unmourned." All too often it is true. In many religious communities people do not know one another's name!

Lack of commitment to others among religious is an anguishing problem. Genuine charity and commitment to others is rare among religious. This causes rivalry, jealousy, emulation. Gabriel Marcel has said, "To exist is to exist with others." Do people really exist in religious communities? Do they really exist with others? This lack of commitment produces an atmosphere of neutral apathy. How often religious hear the kind of "self-protection" maxims that are common among uncommitted men: "Don't go out on a limb, you'll get hurt." Not-getting-hurt is not the absolute. One did not enter religious life never to be hurt. "Don't get involved." Sometimes we do not get involved, and then one sees cases of people like Kitty Genovese: nice Christians sitting quietly and watching someone being murdered. Sometimes this happens in religious communities too. Pious religious sit back and watch other people being murdered, not necessarily with a knife—perhaps with a tongue, perhaps with a decision. They sit and watch and then go off piously to make their examination of conscience as to whether they wore their tassel on the right or on the left that morning.

When a certain ecclesiastic finally decided that civil rights was a moral issue, about twenty years after it was clear to every Christian, a group of nuns who had never said a word in defense of civil rights, under his "protection" went marching in the streets in defense of civil rights. What happened? Was it wrong one day and right the next? What happens in internationally known cases where religious will not support a clearly moral issue? There are many cases like that. These situations indicate, besides moral bankruptcy, immaturity and psychological problems.

There are factors which produce immaturity before, during, and after religious formation. There is the time after the formation, when the nun or the Brother or the priest, or the seminarian, meets the wide world for the first time. Among the most tragic cases are those which occur during the first five years after formation. These crises are not easy to solve. Suddenly a priest decides he never wanted to be a priest. The first question is: "Why did you ever enter?" For a variety of factors, some of which have been already described. It is very common that young professed have crises of sexuality. An individual who lived without problems as a seminarian, or nun, during the period of formation, suddenly after final vows experiences this crisis. This is simply postponed puberty. When religious suddenly begin fornicating or masturbating or engaging in all sorts of other unlikely activities, they may not be actually sinning before God. I am not going to enter into the question of subjective guilt. The fact is that it would be better if they did not do these acts, for their own peace of soul, and for other reasons. The root question is: Why do they do it? It is often nothing but a delayed adolescence. They never received the proper affective training.

Another curious phenomenon to be noticed is a sudden stoppage of work. Religious who worked very hard during their formation suddenly become "compulsive resters." They have to rest fourteen hours a day to gather their strength to rest tomorrow. Or they become compulsive recreators: they are glued to TV or to golf. Nuns do not play golf much now, but they will in another ten years. The fundamental question we must ask is: "Why?" The answer often lies in the fact that the formation was one of pressure and fear. While the pressure was on, religious worked. When the pressure is lifted, they do not. We must also blame the "prize theory": the donkey with the carrot. "If you are a good girl, we will give you this; if you are a good girl, you may get your vows; if you are a good girl, we may send you on to studies." The carrot is held before the donkey for years. Suddenly the donkey has eaten the whole carrot and stares out to reality. What is left? She decides, "I do not want to be a nun." It is better to keep the carrot away from her nose from the beginning and let her decide these factors personally.

There are also reasons in the period after formation, which produce frustration, conflict, and neurosis. These frustrations fall into three categories: the intellectual, the moral, the spiritual.

Let me begin with the intellectual. A Superior tells a subject he must get a doctorate. The subject works, exhausts himself, changes many personal attitudes to become a scholar—and gets his doctorate. It is the will of obedience, of God. As soon as he gets it, he is put into work where he could not possibly use a doctorate. Meanwhile another religious, with no degree, is told, "Now you do not have to take those dirty jobs: give them to the young Ph.D." This produces conflict. The same is true if one is trained to be a high school teacher and suddenly is told to run bazaars or something equally absurd. A nun is trained to be a hospital nun. She learns, perhaps with particular competence, bacteriology, and then is told, "We do not need a bacteriologist at the moment: we need an accountant." This causes frustration. If an Order cannot put a religious to do the work he or she has been trained to do, the Order must cut down on its works. Religious must learn this. They must cut works to the bone. They should be concerned with high quality work and with the religious family as such. One religious group has twenty-eight colleges across the country. They should abandon all of them except four. Then they will be able to treat religious subjects as religious instead of as telephone plugs: pull out this, plug in that—one plug is the same size as the other. Human beings do not act that way, nor do they react well to such treatment.

There is often a conflict between professional work and religious life. A hospital nun has a social service vocation. She entered to serve the poor. She is sent to a hospital. No one but the rich can get into this hospital to begin with; she is not serving the poor. Secondly, her job is to be an accountant, which any qualified atheist could do much better than she. This produces an inner conflict. Religious also often experience lip service to values, i.e., lies—lip service, untruth, instrumentalizations of values. A nun gets a degree in surgery. She is a surgeon, but the Superior decides the Order needs someone to be a hospital helper, to empty pots. Sister Doctor finds herself doing this work. This simply means that there is no genuine inner respect for the Christian values of learning. There is no respect for truth. There is no respect for value. This can and does cause conflicts.

An exaggerated professionalism which is creeping into religious life today can also cause a great deal of conflict. What is meant by exaggerated professionalism? Religious must be trained to be as efficient as they can in their work. On the other hand, Superiors must remember that they are primarily dealing with religious, not doctors or surgeons or nurses. Primarily a religious group is a religious family. If there are some in the family who have not been trained, because of the malice or stupidity of previous Superiors, to a proper degree of competence, one cannot crush them. They too are religious. This one sees very often, and very often the injustice is little short of criminal. When a nun was twenty, she wanted to take a surgeon's degree, and was told: "Do not be silly, we will never need that." Now, when she is forty, Superiors turn around and say, "Where is your surgeon's degree? We need one. You have not got one. What can we do with you?" This is scarcely a religious way of acting, but it is hardly uncommon. This is a professionalism which is exaggerated; it causes neuroses.

There are tremendous conflicts which arise in the religious life because of the bad preparation of the nun, priest, or Brother. If a nun is put to teach mathematics and realizes that three in the class know ten times as much mathematics as she, every hour in the class causes profound strain. One should not assign her to mathematics without proper training.

There is also a conflict which arises after formation caused by disagreement with authority. This can only be solved by a generous attempt on both sides to come to a charitable understanding of what authority is. A person who really has authority almost never uses it. Authority does not impose. The good Superior tries more and more to avoid ever imposing anything on anyone. The suggestions come from the "inferior," "what I would like to do." They are listened to; one consults with them and makes the best of the situation. Both sides yield to a certain extent. The old nineteenth-century ideal of "it is *my will* that you do this" is gone and dead. It would never work with today's religious. It did not with the older generation either. They festered underneath. They did what Superiors said, but as Superiors know, there is no one like a religious for doing everything that the Superior says and frustrating his will at the same time. It is better not to impose one's will that way. There has also been a failure in the past on the part of Superiors to express their genuine will. They kept the subject often in an ambivalent situation. They told him, "Oh, you must write; it is your vocation to write, write more books, write more books"; and he said, "Splendid, could I have a little time?" "Oh, we're awfully sorry about that, we can't give you any time or any secretaries or any help or anything." The subject eventually develops a crisis. "What am I supposed to be? To do?"

With nuns and priests there are crises that occur because their group fails to adapt quickly enough. What has to be adapted must be adapted rapidly, but not, of course, without experimentation. However, one cannot wait fifty years to experiment or one will not have any personnel to experiment with.

There is also a crisis in the intellectual order that centers around the problem of how to integrate the intellectual life with the spiritual.

How is one to do intellectual work and become a contemplative? Robert Bellarmine had that problem. There are intellectual conflicts in the community between different age groups and between the conservatives and the liberals. This conflict is not new; it is ancient. The only solution to it is openness, dialogue, charity.

There are also, surprisingly enough, moral conflicts in the religious life. What do I mean by moral conflicts? I refer to such conflicts as cause a religious to feel that he does not know where he is at in the moral order, as happens when a priest or a nun is forbidden by Superiors to demonstrate for Christian values, such as civil rights. Seminarians are ordered to help break a legitimate strike. This often creates a moral conflict in a thinking man who is religious. These conflicts are very common today; they are genuine moral conflicts, where a person feels that he is not permitted by his religious group to be even a Christian, much less a religious.

There are moral conflicts which arise when religious are forced to do immoral acts, wicked, evil acts. A religious does not have to obey when he is ordered to sin, but many religious think that sin consists in violating one commandment only. There are others. Let me give hypothetical examples. Let us suppose that a nurse is unjustly dismissed by the administrator of a hospital, but Sister Jane is underneath the administrator. If she opposes the administrator, she will be in Hoshkosh next year. She does not have the qualifications to work in Hoshkosh, or the health, or the desire. It is a terrible, agonizing problem. How far does she go in trying to see the Superior's point of view? How far does she go in trying to mask for herself that in this mortal sin against justice, she is a material and perhaps a formal collaborator? Let us suppose that Sister President decides to hire ten professors, because the college will be evaluated next year.

Everyone knows and I know perfectly well, as dean, that all of these ten professors are going to be dismissed next year, after the college is evaluated. I am told, of course, not to tell them this. I help to uproot the lives of ten families, wives, children, all. This is, of course, a gross sin against charity and justice for which I will probably go to hell. But what can I do? If I say anything I will not only be in conflict, I probably will not be around to be in conflict. I will be digging wells in Alaska.

What does one do when someone deforms or attacks the character of another, but cannot do anything about it? Let us suppose that a benefactor of the community systematically, deliberately, over a long period of time assassinates the character of one of the religious in the house. All are aware of the malice, the harm done, but also that the benefactor will cease benefactions if I protest. Moreover, my Superior has indicated that I should not only not protest, but, by public honors to the "benefactor," lend credence to the campaign. These situations cause moral conflicts.

Suppose a religious was in a situation where he had to collaborate with injustice. Suppose he had actively to collaborate with a Superior who was a pathological liar, as occurs. Suppose a situation develops where the editor of a magazine is told to print an editorial which contains lies because his Superior wanted him to print it. Will he print it, or will he not? He may be out of a job if he does not print it, and he is trained only for this job. It is very easy to advise not to print it, but what does the religious do the next day? He is not prepared to dig. What does he do?

Let me posit a mythical situation in which Superior X appoints Monk Y to the task of spiritual adviser to young boys. Monk Y, as superabundant evidence from scores of boys makes clear, is an overt and persuasive homosexual. However, when the Dean points this out, Father Superior points out that Monk Y brings in great sums of money and must not be upset.

What if one is required to collaborate with financial lies? Suppose that the provincial wants to build a university which costs 60 million dollars. He describes his financial assets to his Superior in lying terms. The procurator underneath him has to sign the lies. The only thing the "inferior" is trained for is procuratorship. If he refuses to sign the lies, he is out. Where? God knows. If he signs the lies, 60 million dollars is likely to vanish. It has happened. What does one do? Suppose one is required to collaborate with stealing— naturally one should call it by more polite names! Suppose a donor gives a college one hundred thousand dollars for recreational facilities for the nuns. Mother General decides to build a student dormitory with the money, and put in one large recreation room which the nuns may use when the girls are not using it, e.g., from 1 p.m. to 8 a.m. This is theft. Suppose one were on the Council, and had to approve this. What does one do?

Often there are moral problems which create great conflict for the individual religious who has a conscience. Some problems are caused by the hypocrisy that is at times rampant in religious life. Suppose that in a group of religious the superior distributed two dollars a week for carfare knowing that every religious used and needed ten. Where do they get the other eight? Somewhere. This type of hypocrisy can cause great problems. One major conflict is the conflict of work versus prayer. Superiors say: you must pray an hour a day or four hours, whatever the rule requires; then the Superior assigns a nun a schedule that will not allow her to pray ten minutes a day. This sort of ambiguity can tear religious apart. What are the solutions to all this? First, religious, too, must cultivate the natural virtues and the moral virtues. The fact that one is a religious does not exempt him from the natural law. The ten commandments still bind him. Before the institute, the ten commandments still bind him. He cannot lie; he cannot steal; he cannot defame people's characters; he has to observe the natural law; he has to be a good Christian. There is also nothing wrong with cultivating natural virtues, such as courtesy, good breeding. Genuine honest charity is a great solver of problems.

Many problems would be solved if religious selected Superiors carefully and never repeated them, for their sake and for the sake of the group. Especially should one never repeat them immediately after office. They should not be kept in too long. It is a tragedy for them and for others. Above all, religious should avoid any chain of spiritual Lesbianism or homosexuality, where father or mother picks out a whole succession of children and grandchildren, and great-grandchildren, and installs them as Superiors. One should change the atmosphere, getting a new breath every three or six years. If Mother Superior recommends someone, let us for that very reason choose someone else, just to get a change. We should also remove even the most competent Superiors as soon as our institute allows us to. If the institute allows us to remove them in three years, remove them in three years. As everyone else, religious tend to freeze in their patterns. Superiors are also very isolated. People do not tell Superiors the truth. They often fail to, either through reverential fear or from less noble motives. Superiors' ideas are not challenged enough. Religious should, of course, at once remove incompetent Superiors, but they will rarely do this.

Admit the mistake and remove them, within a day, if necessary, within a week. Religious usually keep up the fraud, saying, "We have to keep them in for their length of term." We have all observed high neurotics kept in for years to preserve "face."

Group therapy would help religious a great deal. Religious should train some of their subjects to be their resident psychiatrists. The fundamental solution depends on charity. Charity is the most important element of the solution of all the problems religious meet.

All too often religious either do not understand authentic religious values, or if they are aware of them intellectually, do not act upon them. Precisely how much of religious training is directed toward spirituality and authentic morality? We might well reflect on this question as we consider alcoholism. There are not many alcoholic nuns, although there are some. Alcoholism is not unknown, nor is drug addiction unknown, among nuns. The ratio may rise consistently as nuns get more freedom.

The ratio of alcoholism among clerics would seem to be 3 to 1 what it is among the lay male population of this country. But that is not precisely my concern. My concern is to analyze the psychological attitudes that lie behind alcoholism, and compare them with genuine religious attitudes. We must then reflect on what kind of formation the cleric may have received, and whether the fault is due to the individual, or partly to his formation. Presumably clerics did not enter clerical or religious life as alcoholics.

The first characteristic of the alcoholic is egocentricity. One of the characteristics of a religious personality is unselfishness, precisely the opposite of egocentricity. What is the fundamental religious orientation of this person?

A second characteristic is low tolerance for tension—what the sociologists call an inability to tolerate tension. On the other hand, religious have heard all through their religious formation that they should be patient people, imitating the patience of Christ. How is it that this large group of clerics, three times as large as one would find in the ordinary male population, is characterized by an inability to tolerate small difficulties. What was their spiritual formation?

A third characteristic of the alcoholic is grandiosity, what one might call in simple, religious language, pride or vanity. But Christians, from Christ's time on, have emphasized humility as a Christian attitude.

A fourth characteristic of the alcoholic is the inability to relate normally, warmly, humanly with other human beings. Yet the fundamental, the primordial virtue of Christianity is charity, which certainly implies an ability to relate warmly and humanly to other human beings.

A fifth characteristic is a sense of omnipotence—the alcoholic feels totally independent of circumstances, people. Yet the first meditation religious make instructs them that they are essentially relative, dependent creatures. They learn to cultivate a sense of metaphysical contingency; they are dependent essentially, related to Another who is omnipotent.

A sixth characteristic is emotional instability and insecurity. It has already been noted that insecurity is the most devastatingly corrosive influence in religious life. Yet religious men are supposed to have a confidence in God which relieves much basic insecurity. They are also supposedly surrounded by an "erosphere," an atmosphere of love from the religious family, which supports their emotional and psychological security. Again we ask the question, "Who and what is responsible?"

A seventh characteristic is irresponsibility. One cannot depend on the alcoholic's arriving on time, doing anything assigned on time. Yet it seems a profoundly religious characteristic to be dependable, to fulfill one's promise, to live up to one's obligations, to accept seriously the commitments one has made. Why, then, does one find that this large proportion of clerics are irresponsible? Is it their religious formation?

An eighth characteristic is lying. One of the most profound human virtues is the virtue of truthfulness. It may be rarer than emeralds, but it is still a Christian virtue.

A ninth characteristic is infancy-behavior, a retreat to that mode of adaptation which was helpful when one was an infant at the breast. And yet religious life, clerical life, priestly life is supposed to bring one to Christian adulthood. We note the contrasts.

A tenth characteristic is uncertain sexuality. Alcoholics do not know, emotionally, whether they are male or female. On the other hand, priestly and religious commitments, virginity and celibacy, should be based upon a maturity in the sexual life which is even greater than that required of the parent.

An eleventh characteristic is the feeling of loneliness and isolation. Yet it seems that, particularly among religious, there should be a genuine sense of community which prevents such loneliness and isolation. However, among young religious today one of the questions most discussed is the question of loneliness in the religious life.

A twelfth characteristic is narcissism or self-admiration. But it is a religious and Christian characteristic to be more or less forgetful of self. Not that this requires an unrealistic evaluation of self. If God made me a genius, I am a genius and I have to put up with the burdens that go with genius-hood. If God made me stupid, I am stupid and I have to put up with the burdens that go with stupidity. That is simple honesty, humility. But religious men and women are not supposed to constantly reflect on their own talents or preen their multi-colored feathers.

A thirteen characteristic is hostility, basic underlying hostility. Fundamentally, alcoholics are filled with hatred and hostility, while on the surface they are the meekest of men or women. Yet Christianity calls upon us not to be aggressive and hostile toward others, but to be loving, open, receptive toward them.

A fourteenth characteristic is "oral dependence" or demandingness. "My wish must be fulfilled the instant before it is expressed." Yet religious men should be humble and also independent in a healthy sense, rather than demanding of others.

A fifteenth characteristic is a *basic* low self-esteem, lack of trust in oneself along with the grandiosity and the pride and the vanity. Yet it is a fundamental Christian attitude to accept oneself as God made one, with all his inabilities, deficiencies, defects, limitations.

What causes alcoholism in the religious life? What psychological and sociological conditions of the religious life foster it? Is the individual responsible, or is it the group atmosphere?

QUESTION. "Please comment on 'the God-is-love orientation,' which emphasizes dialogue and commitment, with minimal recognition of the need to do the tasks which can be escaped in community living, but would have to be faced up to if the individual were living outside?"

ANSWER. By this I presume is meant that there are some religious who are great talkers, but when it comes to charity in practice do nothing. What can we do? We can only hope that they will become psychologically alive to their own limitations, realize that charity requires many unpleasant tasks in daily living. St. John says, "Let us love not in words, but in truth and in deed."

QUESTION. "How do you reconcile the emphasis on 'God in the neighbor' in the life of prayer? God is our source and aim and more than an immediate encounter, is it not so?"

ANSWER. The neighbor is the "sacrament" of God, and this is where we encounter him. If one doesn't love the neighbor whom one sees, one does not love God.

QUESTION. "Does it not seem we are missing many opportunities for experiencing and spreading joy in our religious life—joy in work, in the liturgy, in the very challenges made upon our talents, academic pursuits, and compassion for the needy, because we are bogged down by anxieties?"

ANSWER. Yes. Whoever wrote that question has a very sharp insight. Religious life should be characterized by joy. The only way one will inspire vocations is by reflecting this joy. All the conflicts and difficulties I spoke about before create an anxiety which can submerge this joy. Moreover, one should not overwork religious lest this joy disappear. Most nuns are overworked. Religious need a certain amount of time for relaxation, for tranquility, for recollection, for prayer, for sheer joy in life. If they do not have this, their very faces betray tension, anxiety, nervousness, fatigue, exhaustion, preoccupation. Not having joy, they cannot spread it.

QUESTION. "What makes religious and priests pompous, demanding, tyrannical, selfish, everything they teach others not to be?"

ANSWER. So often we are not fundamentally religious people. We may wear the tassel on the right side; we may have the phylactery where it belongs, but we are not genuinely humble, charitable, loving people. Why? Some of the reasons have been offered.

QUESTION. "I am in a certain year of my religious life. I have seen the situation you describe, and have endured it, suffered it, and seen others crushed under it. However, what matters is that God's work remains undone. I have dutifully accepted this over all the years and done the best I can."

ANSWER. The Church is built on people like you, who see the situation as it is and go on doing their best.

QUESTION. "Would you discuss the idea of 'ecclesial' obedience? In the practice of obedience or in the living of religious life, must there be rules that regulate little details of living, permission to leave the house and stay overnight in the homes of one's relations, to accept an invitation received because of one's profession, to return to the convent at a designated hour?"

ANSWER. Your foundress was not preoccupied with that. She was preoccupied with certain fundamental insights she had about what could and should be done by dedicated women for the poor in the hospitals, in education, in every other work you take up. These little details of religious life should be explicitations of the fundamental motif, of the fundamental insight your foundress or founder had. Let us not blow them up to the point that they become the be-all and end-all of religious life. They are details. As to how they should be formulated: summon the community together and discuss them. If the community wants to change a rule so that one comes in at 11 o'clock at night or 12 o'clock or 1 o'clock at night, let the community change it. Adapt these little things as far as possible. Every Superior of every community should have flexibility. Mother General or Mother Provincial or Father Provincial should not decide every detail of life in every community. The Superior of each community should be a Superior and should regulate these details for this particular house. The rule may be different for each particular house. Flexibility is required.

QUESTION. "I am beginning to wonder what we religious are committed to. If, as I believed twenty years ago, a religious is one who gives his or her whole life to God and to the service of one's fellowman, for the love of God, then I believe we need a drastic restructuring. Our schools are so understaffed and our Sisters so overburdened that any possible benefit students may get from contact with religious is negated."

ANSWER. This is an absolutely fundamental question. It touches one of the nerves in religious life. Religious have grossly overexpanded in a purely materialistic way. We have taken on far too many works, and we are denying the very reasons for which we are founded. For example, a group was founded for excellence in education, and they spread themselves over 27 colleges, every one of which is second-rate. They are denying the very reason for which they went into this apostolate. Cut down the works. Refuse them. If bishops impose them, say no. "I can't do it. I do not have that many nuns, and I will not kill the ones I have."

QUESTION. "Would it not be more realistic for us to maintain a very few good small schools?"

ANSWER. Yes. I do not believe that your foundress wanted large masses of second-rate education.

QUESTION. "What is the best approach to help those who are mentally disturbed?"

ANSWER. It seems that often too little care is given too late. I suggest a resident psychiatrist. We should give them, as far as possible, technical assistance. It is expensive; so is feeding the Sister.

QUESTION. "What about someone who does not want to be helped?"

ANSWER. Sometimes the Superior must insist, because the nun is dragging down the whole community.

QUESTION. "How can we profit by, if not prevent, the mass exodus of Sisters from the community?"

ANSWER. By adopting the suggestions I have given.

QUESTION. "How can we break down the lack of communication between the Brothers and the community administration? Does the community administration really want to be communicated to?"

ANSWER. Oft times, especially with Brothers, but also with priests, religious set up completely phony procedures. For example, they say: "Now we will have community discussion as to whether we should go up the left side or down the left side of the stairs." The Superior starts off; or if he doesn't, he makes it known ahead of time what his opinion is, and no one dares to speak up. If one wants communication, normally he will get it. The same thing is true of a teacher in the classroom. If he does not want communication, he probably will not get it. Subjects have also to be willing to suffer a little and tell Superiors what they think, even when what they think is sure to be unwelcome. This is a very serious problem. If we do not have communication, we will not be around long. No one in modern work is going to live without communication.

QUESTION. "How can those who feel that the community has been too complacent about its past and should make some effort towards restructuring the community, succeed in persuading people to allow limited experimentation, even expecting mistakes?"

ANSWER. Experimentation does not mean we prove the idea is right ahead of time. It means literally that one is experimenting; if one is interested at all in experimentation, he should allow people the liberty to make mistakes, and expect them to make mistakes.

QUESTION. "Will you comment on the nature of true obedience?"

ANSWER. I have done so in my book *To Live Is Christ*, and I comment more frankly in this book.

QUESTION. "We hear a great deal about fulfillment. Is it not interpreted sometimes to mean self-satisfaction?"

ANSWER. Yes, it is. Often! I discussed this when I spoke of exaggerated professionalism. We have to be very careful that our humanism, our fulfillment, is a Christian humanism, which always embraces the mystery of the cross, self-denial, and penance.

QUESTION. "Often we are told there is no love evident in religion today. Do we not sometimes confuse sentiment or emotion with love of preference or love which is in the will?"

ANSWER. Love is not only in the will. It flows out into affectivity and action too. What religious should have is not just that "I wish you good, but don't come near me for any of it" attitude. What they should have is a genuine, warm, family feeling of affection.

QUESTION. "Please comment on obedience. One sometimes gets the impression that it is no longer important, or that it keeps or makes us immature."

ANSWER. In the past it has often kept and made us immature. In the future it will not, because people will not stay under that kind of obedience. Obedience is still necessary and it will always be a fundamental part of religious life, but it has been up-played far too much. Play it down for a while.

QUESTION. "We have been told for some time that we must consider people as persons. Does this apply to everyone but Superiors?"

ANSWER. There is nothing against the natural law in loving Superiors. It also helps if they are lovable. It is true that, partially because of the fault of our structure, religious tend to isolate Superiors. They do not even talk to them, or encourage them; they leave them in their ivory tower. Superiors, too, are human beings; they, too, need affection, understanding, sympathy.

QUESTION. "Many Sisters are uneasy about what seems to be too much concern about externals and non-essentials, that is, spending money, design of dress, and not enough concern about genuine renewal."

ANSWER. I agree with those many Sisters.

QUESTION. "Does it seem that the structure of the novitiate should be radically changed?"

ANSWER. I think it should be almost abolished.

QUESTION. "Is there a possibility that with the development of clinical psychology, specifically religious and ascetical formation will become less important?"

ANSWER. There is a fundamental insight here. There is a parallelism between the two, the natural and supernatural. A genuine religious value promotes the genuine psychological values of the person, and a genuine psychological growth promotes the genuine religious values of the person. Those who are doing the real ethical work today are often not the moral theologians and the ethicians, but the psychologists. The psychiatrists claim they have no interest in morals. But they urge the client, while declaiming all interest in morals, toward a genuinely moral life, because they wish to aid the client to be a genuinely human person.

QUESTION. "From a tender age on, I taught at a certain high school. A vigilant, protective senior Sister had some reservations regarding my popularity. I recall asking, at the time, how old does a Sister have to be to be a woman? I sometimes now reflect how naïve I must have been. Thirty years later I still am the same little school girl."

ANSWER. This is too often tragically true of many nuns and priests. God wants you to be adult. If the religious life, as it is lived concretely, does not produce adults, God does not want it to continue to exist. How does one produce adults? One must constantly give them increasing responsibility, tend to their individuality, let them make their mistakes. One must let them grow at their own pace. One has to collaborate with their own inner being, not force on them what we want to make out of them.

QUESTION. "So much is said about the matter of maturity today. Would you please give us a clear definition of it."

ANSWER. Maturity is the ability to live and to love within the framework of stratified reality in all its complexities.

Question. "In many books I read the phrase 'the full, integrated, completely human person.' Specifically, how does a person reach this integration, this completion of himself? Integration is a wonderful phrase, but what does it really mean?"

ANSWER. It means the ability to cope with reality as it is, to be at ease with reality, to feel one can cope with it, to be mature enough to love within the structure of reality. If a man is married and has ten children, it is not within the structure of reality that a nun should develop a conjugal love for him, or a love which, while remaining chaste, is still within the conjugal structure. To be mature is to be able to live and to love within the complicated complex structure of reality.

QUESTION. "Could you say something about vocation as theology views it today?"

ANSWER. God, Christ, simply calls us to be ourselves, in the fullness of ourselves. It remains for us to respond to this call in a way which brings about this fullness. We select the life which will open to us human fulfillment, Christian fulfillment, supernatural fulfillment.

QUESTION. "Will you please clarify the Code of Canon Law regarding electioneering and campaigning for chapter members and members of the Council?"

ANSWER. I do not know that Canon Law has much to say about it. I do not think there is anything in most institutes, or in the natural law, which would forbid one's expressing a viewpoint and discussing people who are capable of certain tasks. One is supposed to know something about the person he is voting for. One should not buy votes by giving people positions if they vote for a candidate. Yet one must discuss the candidates' qualifications.

QUESTION. "Why is it that some religious look upon experimentation with horror?"

ANSWER. Be patient. People who have been in a religious community for years have been formed in certain ways. One cannot throw off the habits of a lifetime, habits of thought, action, sentiment, devotion, which were all built into a person as part and parcel of religious commitment.

QUESTION. "There is little communication between age-groups in our community. What can we do about it?"

ANSWER. This is a problem which only charity will solve. Do you understand what older nuns have gone through, what they have suffered? Some young people have no sense of history. They wonder why it is that Sister Agatha, who is eighty, doesn't understand Teilhard de Chardin. Realize what a formation she had. She did not have the formation or advantages the young religious had. She also bore and endured things which young religious would perhaps find impossible to bear and endure. Have enough charity to realize that people cannot change their ideas easily. On the other hand, older nuns, or the ones who are by temperament conservative, should realize that all that is under ninety is not evil. The young have the same difficulties, more or less, that the old have. They express them differently. They are not out to destroy an institute. They are determined to discover what its fundamental spirit is. Let both see if they cannot come together and find the elements of wisdom in each other's point of view. The community must be united, and only through dialogue and charity are religious going to unite. It cannot be accomplished without genuine charity.

QUESTION. "Do you think it is necessary to have experimentation concerning other factors than habits?"

ANSWER. Habit experimentation is the most superficial experimentation of all. Religious have to experiment, under the control of their Superior, and with their discreet advice on a great many things—the apostolate, for example. Will you be in hospital work twenty years from now? Will you be in the kind of educational work you are in now? One has to experiment, under the control of Superiors, in every phase of the religious life. That is what the Church is asking for. New ideas should be proposed by individuals, groups, the community, to the Superior, receive her reaction, proposed to higher Superiors and, with modifications, engaged in, mistakes made, withdrawals made, and further experiments made. Every aspect of religious life has to be submitted to this process. Otherwise religious are going to be nonexistent.

QUESTION. "I am of the opinion that it is necessary to love humanly before we can love God."

ANSWER. You cannot love God if you do not love man. Read St. John. He says it point-blank. A man, he says, who says he loves God, whom he does not see, and does not love his brother, whom he does see, the same is a liar. One must love humanly, yes. But this love must be realistic. One does not indulge in a conjugal love for someone one cannot marry. That is not realistic, adult. It is not adult when a secretary indulges in that kind of love for her married employer. It is not adult either to indulge in an emotional, tense, sexual-deviational love for a fellow religious. But we must love men, and women, human beings. Religious must have friends of both sexes. Men religious must have women friends. Women religious must have men friends, if they are going to be adults. This opinion, heterodox for many years, was finally confirmed at one great Order's general congregation. Having had such opinions for the last thirty years, I was pleased to see a retroactive approval of my wickedness. I cannot insist too strongly that the essence of the Christian life is charity, genuine human love of others, having regard, naturally, for all the things that moralists have told us over the years. We simply must have dear friends.

QUESTION. "Presuming a woman is not abnormally neurotic when she enters religious life, but becomes such, partially because of the system, is it fair and just to dismiss her or even encourage her to leave the community?"

ANSWER. In some institutes one is forbidden to do that. If a religious enters, takes public vows, one cannot dismiss him because he requires psychiatric care for the rest of his seventy-nine years. What should one do in the concrete?

Should one encourage him to leave? One should offer psychological or psychiatric help, if he is willing to accept it. It is fair enough to propose the alternative of leaving, if one honestly believes that this will help him become less neurotic. One should take care of him as long as he insists on staying in. Eventually the psychiatrist will tell him that it is best to leave. These matters have to be delicately handled. I do not believe that as soon as one sees he is going to have to spend money on a subject, he should send him out. On the other hand I do not believe one should encourage such a neurotic subject to stay.

QUESTION. "Has not the community a responsibility to him?"

ANSWER. Certainly. However, there are also the normal members of the community to consider. One cannot load a community with eight percent neurotics. There would be ninety-nine percent the following year. A normal person cannot live with neurotics and remain sane. The pressures are too great.

QUESTION. "Many are neurotic in religious life; all of us are neurotic to some degree. Should we get rid of all neurotics after 20, 30, 40 years in the community?"

ANSWER. No. As long as they keep their neurosis in control and do not irritate other people too much, they should be kept, if they wish to remain.

QUESTION. "If there are places where acknowledged neurotics live and create tension for those who are normal, what can be done for the community?"

ANSWER. The only solution is to distribute them. This may

sound harsh, but one has to find a place for them in different communities, rather than lumping them all together. Do not impose them on the aged, as some groups do. Try to find out where they think they would fit in most peaceably. Consult them. Consult the Superior of the house. Do not put too many in one community.

QUESTION. "Should a Sister recovering from mental illness, that is, nervous breakdowns, be put back into a classroom of slow learners?"

ANSWER. Sister should be put back in the work *of her choice*. Superiors should consult subjects. Every effort should be made to readjust the religious to life with the greatest peace and ease. Everyone is aware that Superiors labor under very great difficulties. They have to fill certain positions. They are often forced into impossible situations because of the numerous works they have taken on. But rather than risk another nervous breakdown, one should let this Sister do whatever she feels she can do.

QUESTION. "How does one cope with a problem like the following: The community I live with is under great strain. This has been made known to higher authorities. The only answer we have received is that we should pray, and perhaps something can be done."

ANSWER. We should pray.

QUESTION. "This Superior is in her second term of office."

ANSWER. I do not believe in second terms. It is a bad index of your congregation if you must repeat Superiors. If you cannot find prudent, generous, intelligent Superiors without repeating them, you should give up.

QUESTION. "Do not we religious often have the tendency to feel that we will break down authority if we admit we made a mistake in appointing a Superior?"

ANSWER. If I put in a Superior who proves impossible, I do not destroy authority by taking that Superior out: I foster authority. No one will have any respect for authority if I do not take her out. Superiors are reluctant to do this. They want to, as the Japanese say, "save face," and will often save face at the cost of the entire community or province. I have seen Superiors under psychiatric care at the head of great institutions. Why? To remove them before their stated six years would "hurt" the man, who is now hurting 500 other men. Secondly, it might suggest that I was incompetent for having put him in. I have known places where this exists and where Superiors refuse to act year after year after year.

QUESTION. "What is your opinion of a day structured as follows: Rise at 5:30; eat at 6:05; work and manual labor 7:30 to 10; breakfast on the run; canonical training 10:15 until 11; manual labor again until 2:30; free time for a half an hour; class 3:30 to 4:30; manual labor again; dinner on the run."

ANSWER. Something has gone wrong. That Brother is over-worked.

QUESTION. "What is your opinion of night silence?"

ANSWER. We used to have it, and it was considered sacro-sanct. Things have changed. Now young religious can go to the TV room until 2 or 3 in the morning if they wish and chat or watch TV. They are told, "The responsibility is yours. You have to be up in the morning attending difficult classes. You are supposed to be a religious. We leave the responsibility to you." Some customs like night silence can be a great aid to prayer. Some can pray well after listening to the late late show and arise early the next morning to meditate. Many cannot. However, night silence is not the most essential element of religious life. Let the community decide, under the guidance of a local Superior, with the consent of the higher Superior, what one should do about night silence.

QUESTION. "In the interest of 'self-fulfillment and individuality,' is it not possible to rationalize about charity as opposed to required night silence?"

ANSWER. If a fellow religious comes in to talk during sacred night silence, should one dismiss her? No. If she comes in three nights in a row, delicately suggest to her that you tire easily, especially of her. Night silence is a good thing, but it is not an absolute that can never be infringed upon.

QUESTION. "What do you think of having young Sisters closely associated with old Sisters, working in old age homes and hospitals for retired Sisters?"

ANSWER. I presume that young Sisters would be closely associated with older Sisters all during their religious life. I presume that every community would have a certain complement of old Sisters and young Sisters, if young religious keep entering.

QUESTION. "What do you think of assigning young Sisters to work exclusively with old Sisters?"

ANSWER. This would be a considerable strain on younger Sisters. It is a great joy for older Sisters to have cheerful, generous, young nuns who work well with older people.

While it is a great lift to the older Sisters, I would not *impose* this assignment on young nuns. I would not assign a young Sister to this work over a long period of time, if she found it a psychological strain. I do feel great sympathy with religious who have borne the burden and the heat of the day, and are shunted off in a corner where no one has an interest in them. How can this be an expression of family devotion? No matter how difficult older religious are, they still belong to the family. If a group is to remain religious, they must have a family structure and love for all age groups.

QUESTION. "We talk and learn about the equality and freedom of men. Why do some Sisters feel that the Negro should not be free to live as others? Often when they speak about the Negroes, they refer to them as 'niggers.'"

ANSWER. That is, of course, disgraceful. We must admit that one of the greatest blots on the history of the American Church is our having waited until the civil government took steps about civil liberties. We, who claim to be founded by Jesus Christ and to have illumination and guidance from the Holy Spirit, what did we do?

QUESTION. "You suggested that communities of more than twenty are really not communities. Can you suggest ways of breaking up large houses into smaller communities to promote communication and charity?"

ANSWER. Yes. Build complexes, small houses around a central building, where there is a chapel, a central dining room, and a few other central facilities.

QUESTION. "It is also a question of economics."
ANSWER. Yes, it is.

QUESTION. "What about the large convents already built to house religious communities?"

ANSWER. One can try to sell them, or to convert them into other uses, e.g., student dormitories. There are many practical difficulties in doing this, but it must be the *ideal* toward which religious strive.

QUESTION. "Have you any suggestions as to how a congregation of 750 members might experiment in new forms of community life?"

ANSWER. I wonder if a congregation should have 750 members. Perhaps they should divide. Experiment with new forms of community life? The simplest way is to have the ideas come up from the religious who are living in the community. The religious should submit, in informal discussion with their Superior, their ideas on experimentation in community life. The Superior gathers these ideas, discusses them, rediscusses them, difficulties are brought forth and ironed out, and then the Superior proposes all to a higher Superior. Experimentation is risky, but then life is not without risks.

QUESTION. "How important is experimentation?"

ANSWER. Very important. Without it religious will not be here in a few more years.

QUESTION. "Should we risk what we have already achieved for something that might fail?"

ANSWER. Experimentation does not mean that one rejects tradition. One experiments within the guiding charismatic insights of the founder or foundress, and takes the risks that implies.

EIGHT · FIDELITY

WITH THE RAPID changes taking place in the structures of religious life today, many religious find themselves lost, bewildered, even frightened. Devotions and devotional practices which once created a specific religious atmosphere in a group are dropped, ignored, sometimes ridiculed. The minutiae of religious life which once gave form to a particular style of living are all being challenged. Old apostolates, to which many have given their entire lives, are altered or dropped. As a result some who have neither the training, the aptitude, nor the temperament for the new ones feel displaced. Frequently, in the new cadres developed they are literally unemployable, although jobs may be created for them. It seems as though all aspects, and even the essentials of the religious life, are questioned, probed, challenged. The tight bonds of community life are being gradually loosened, to some, it seems, dissolved. The old certainties and the old securities are gone. It is painful to see the sadness that afflicts many religious as they wonder who erred, how they went wrong, what, if anything, could have been done and was not. A pervasive sense of failure can touch the lives of many in a difficult transitional period. Lives that have been marked by enormous generosity can suddenly find all called in question. Many wonder if they have been betrayed by their congregation, or if they themselves have betrayed the best interests of the congregation and the Church. It is important to realize that the need for change implies no contempt for the achievements of the past, for the sacrifice, ardor, staggering work of the past. Religious have served well the Church and God. No one who has dealt with them,

237

across the world, can fail to note the untiring zeal, the selfless generosity, the fidelity to the Lord's will, as they see it, that marks religious as a whole. Perhaps today, more than anything else, they need to recall that the Lord, too, is faithful. Whatever mistakes have been made, whatever defects have been present, in the group and the individual, the Lord remains faithful. Defective insight, incomplete, partial fidelity mark the human condition. The God of revelation is aware of this, and it does not alter the fidelity of Him in whom there is neither change nor shadow of alteration. All Christians need to ponder deeply and often this unchanging fidelity, and religious are no exception.

The New Testament does not so fully underscore the idea of God's fidelity to man—God's steadfast loyalty to sinful man—as does the Old Testament.

The New Testament underscores God's tenderness, God's love, but not that precise aspect of his rocklike steadfast loyalty to man against all obstacles from man's side which the Old Testament calls His fidelity. Yet this insight is a necessary element in man's spiritual life if he is to preserve himself from an atmosphere of fear in his relationship with God. If the Christian is to preserve himself from an atmosphere of constriction, where his religion does not expand his potentialities, but contracts them, he needs to understand God's fidelity. Particularly in our age, which is an age of double anxiety, existential and neurotic, an understanding of God's fidelity is absolutely necessary if the Christian is to have a balanced approach to the spiritual life.

Man lives today in an age of existential anxiety. He is in a constant position of anxiety: the natural, free communication, free rhythm of coexistence with nature and with himself and other men is lost. He also suffers from neurotic anxiety. The peculiar stress and structure of society produces in the Christian an insecurity that gnaws at the depths of his personality. A grasp of the concept of God's fidelity is an antidote to this. It is only man's intense personal conviction of God's fidelity—fidelity against all obstacles that we present to Him—that can create the authentic climate of Christian life. One sees all sorts of other climates produced in Christian life—an anxiety for perfectionism has often produced inauthentic Christian living. Perfectionism, striving for perfection, is not the central theme or the authentic spiritual climate of Christianity. Creativity and freedom, expansiveness, joy, reliance upon an unchanging love on the part of God, despite all obstacles, this is Christianity's authentic climate. This theme, properly understood, protects the religious against various false emphases in the Christian life, against, for example, emphasis that makes sinlessness the ideal of Christian perfection. An understanding of God's fidelity also protects the religious against legalism, against a fear of the law—not realizing that the law is simply an instrument to demonstrate love and a guidepost to us as to how to return love. At times we meet religious who are unable to accept dispensation from the law, even if legitimately granted. This legalism constricts and narrows our approach to God. Law has a value, but it is not the unique absolute. Moreover, an understanding of God's fidelity to us protects us from that infantilism, that childishness, not childlikeness, which makes us obey out of fear. I will speak here of an unusual theme: God's obligations to man.

To speak of God's obligations may seem, at first glance, rather contradictory. It is, however, theologically correct, founded on the opening message of the Old Testament, a message that resounds throughout the Old Testament.

Christians start their lives with instructions on their obligations toward the living, true, and personal God. Those obligations exist. Christians are taught a sense of duty; they have obligations; they must accept a structure of laws, must obey God's will. Having grasped that, they develop a healthy, tough, virile, responsible, Christian life, a purposeful life. They grasp God's call through the network, the structure of law—ecclesiastical law, moral law, the ten commandments, the commandments of the Church, canonical law. God's invitations are formalized for them, finitized for them in law. The great Christian insights are brought down to encompass lowly man, so that he can understand. Christians vow each day their fidelity to God. They work at the Christian life through this structure of obligation, and this will never be thrown over because Sacred Scripture underscores, over and over again, that the Lord our God is one, is unique, is transcendent, the only God, and demands our obedience to His law. His summons, His demands are absolute; we must do our human best to fulfill them. He is unlike any created person; He is beyond categories. He is unique. What He calls upon man to do, howsoever difficult, man must fulfill. When He manifests His will, the Christian's submission must be absolute. Man never has the right to call Him to the bar of human reason. Man never has the right to judge the living God, *whatever* He demands, even if it be the sacrifice of Isaac. He has only to say "yes," to assent. This is man's role. We are creatures, we submit, we obey—we "keep faith" with the living God. That is the tradition the religious was brought up in, and it is still authentic, still needed today, because today, more than ever, duty is not respected. There exists today a hatred of "legalism," but legalism is not law, and law is not legalism. Legalism is the absolutization of law, and law is not the absolute. It is a signpost, a guide, but it is not the last word. Even if legalism is hated today, the Christian must still face the obligation to observe and love the law of the Lord.

Today we need especially to underscore our duty of fidelity, because the juridical sphere seems rejected by younger Christians. It should not be. The Christian should certainly refuse to make the juridical sphere the norm of Christian virtue. But legalism is not always pharisaism, as some seem to think. Today's emphasis on personalism, when it implies a rejection of discipline, does not aid the religious to come to Christian maturity. The emphasis laid in times past upon duty and observance of the law, fulfillment of obligation, is valid. But that is by far the least important side of the coin.

The other and infinitely more consoling side of the coin is God's fidelity, His obligations to the Christian. The first index of God's willingness to assume these obligations is man's baptism. When the Christian is baptized, God, literally, though we have great difficulty in accepting God literally—God swears an oath to the Christian, personally and individually. All men realize the solemnity of an oath. Many Christians have heard the oath sung at a priest's ordination—"I have sworn an oath: you are a priest forever, according to the order of Melchisidech." There God assures the new priest that he is accepted as a priest until eternity. That is an oath sworn on the part of the personal and living God to the priest.

So, too, at baptism God swears to each Christian an oath. He obliges Himself—the Christian obviously has no rights to make demands upon the living God, but He makes demands upon Himself—He obliges Himself—in all sincerity to give the Christian all that is required throughout his entire Christian existence to come to perfection. At baptism God engages Himself to the Christian in a fashion very much like the marriage vows. The Old Testament says this: God engages Himself to man in a union like that of marriage. He vows Himself in an interpersonal union to each Christian. He takes on at that point a constancy toward the Christian, a love which is a *reliable* love. There is no question of shifting behavior on His part. There is no question of His behavior being dependent upon man's behavior. There is no question of God's fidelity being dependent on man's fidelity to Him. His fidelity is utterly and completely independent of man's fidelity. It is a continuous stable mode of behavior to which the living God has sworn Himself. He will live by His oath *however man behaves*. This is cause for considerable reflection. The idea could create a completely new climate in man's relationships with God. The scriptural word which describes the fidelity of God to man is *chesed*. The translations for this word, none of them is perfect, suggest steadfast love, loving-kindness, fidelity. Fidelity is a good translation because it implies a notion of unchanging, unweary loyalty. God's fidelity simply stands there, no matter what man does, no matter how many attacks man makes on it. Should one call *chesed* "loving-kindness"? Yes, because it is not simply an impersonal fidelity, but it is a special kind of fidelity, a gentle, warm, perservering fidelity. As men grow older in human existence, they begin to realize how grateful they are to friends who are genuinely "kind," thoughtful. The Dutch Canon uses of God the expression "thoughtful and enduring God." Which of us would ever have imagined these words to describe the omnipotent God? "Thoughtful"—this is the way men think of their friends, "thoughtful—enduring —patient"—*chesed* implies that God is a thoughtful and enduring God.

Another expression the Old Testament uses to intimate God's *chesed* is the "forgivingness" of God—He is endlessly forgiving. Another translation often used for *chesed* is "tenderness." It betrays His (if I may use the expression) warm-heartedness. Another implication of *chesed*, which is the central theme of Israel's relationship to God, is the idea of "loyalty"—our God is a *loyal* friend, a friend who stands by when things are good and who stands by when things are less good. The relationship between man and God is best described by "loyalty."

Another implication of *chesed*, however, is that God is "patient"; this is very much like the notion of an "enduring" God. After one has offended Him once, He is still there; after one has offended Him the thousandth time, He is still there. On His part, nothing has altered in the relationship of love He extends to the Christian. But with all these loving expressions—steadfast-love, loving-kindness, forgiveness, loyalty, patience—there are two more: He is an "attentive" God; He knows ahead of time what will please us; and He is a "pious" God, a "considerate" God, the kind of God who knows the small elements in our human life, the shifts in mood and in our feelings from one day to another, who is considerate, a kind of quality we do not often mark in our relationships with the Lord. Yet with *all* these expressions, one must never forget that the word *chesed* contains one fundamental element underlying all, a peculiar understratum to these loving words—the element of toughness, hardness. This *chesed* love, this kind of patience, of consideration, attentiveness, loyalty, loving-kindness, is all based upon the toughness of a love which can resist human shocks. It stands there. We Christians, we religious, of course, are the ones who give the shocks. *Chesed* love is always there. The basic element in the word, an unwearying fidelity, a tireless fidelity, it is at the heart of Israel's relations to God. The basic idea of *chesed* is unquestionably *strength*.

Chesed therefore implies fidelity combined with an unchanging, unwearying tenderness and strength. The Septuagint translated the word as *eleos* or mercy; the Christian knows it, in the Vulgate, and in the English, as "mercy." But mercy only translates half of the richness of the word, the concept. The idea is infinitely wider than that. *Chesed* is, moreover, a love, a tenderness, that, as Jeremiah points out, includes the just, which is very consoling, but also the unjust, us. It extends to all men: it is a love that rests on a firm basis, a *publicly* acknowledged base. That is why God's fidelity is so often compared to marriage vows. When a man marries and takes his marriage vows, he makes a public acknowledgement, before society, that he has committed himself to the other. Society expects constancy in that relationship. The same element is implied in the word *chesed*. God's relationship to man is constantly, throughout the Old Testament, compared to the marriage relationship. However, God's love is not like ours; His fidelity is not like ours, for the simple reason that infidelity on our part does not alter His fidelity in the slightest. Sin, on our part, does not alter God's fidelity. It does not wear it down. We are perfectly aware of the limitations that human love has. We are well aware of how we can be worn down; God, however, cannot; His fidelity cannot be worn down. The fact that Israel was unfaithful to Him—and God knows that she was repeatedly, publicly, scandalously, flagrantly unfaithful— did not alter in the slightest the fact that God had taken a vow to Israel. He must be faithful to His vows; His fidelity to Israel did not change in the slightest. The fact that one partner, Israel, was unfaithful in this marriage relationship did not release God from His obligations. This "determined loyalty," this *chesed*, is an *unconditioned* engagement. I do not know whether any human being is capable of this kind of engagement, where once and forever he commits himself, with the certainty that this engagement will never change whatever the partner's relationship to them becomes. But that is what God's *chesed* is, an *unconditional* engagement.

In the later Old Testament the emphasis on God's fidelity shifts from Israel to the individual. The earlier Old Testament stresses the central notion of God's fidelity to all of Israel, His bride. In later Old Testament revelation the emphasis moves from the group to the individual, to *me* with all my personal history, personal limitations, personal tragedies, personal sin. In the later Old Testament there is no depersonalization: God's fidelity is to each Israelite. This fidelity is never withdrawn, even when the individual is unfaithful. To bring this home to men, God multiplies images. He is a teacher and He expands, develops, this theme. There is, in fact, a sense throughout the Old Testament of almost a search on the part of God as to how to bring this concept of His fidelity home to men. He describes Himself, for example, as a father. Jeremiah already anticipates the beautiful story of the prodigal son. In Jeremiah, fidelity is mentioned in the content of the relationship of father to son. Jeremiah is faithful to his son. The son was by no means faithful to Jeremiah. But the father-image is not unique. The Lord goes further. In Isaiah He appeals to the concept of a mother's love. In Isaiah's "can a woman forget the child of her womb? But if she could, I *cannot* forget you," God explains His faithful love. He uses the concept of the shepherd, whose care for his sheep causes him to risk his life for love of the individual sheep. Jahweh multiplies images to bring home to humanity that He is sincere about His fidelity. One sees this in the very first lines He speaks to Moses, "Go and tell your people that I am the God of your Fathers"; and Moses says, "But we want to know who you are, what is your name." He tells Moses His name, "I am who am." Although there are a thousand interpretations of that phrase, many scholars believe today that God is saying "I am the one who is *with* you." "To be *with* you" does not simply mean presence, it means "I am with you all the way, I am *for* you, I am completely at your disposal." This is God's definition, His name. He is endlessly, completely, totally, unwearingly, committed to mankind.

As the Old Testament develops, we see a gradual enlargement of this beautiful concept of fidelity, *chesed*. At first God had to educate His people, and He expressed the concept of fidelity more in terms of *covenant*-love—He made a contract with Israel: "they will be my people, I will be their God"; they fulfill His law, He will protect them, be with them, defend them against all comers. A certain contractual, almost legal element was emphasized in the earlier days. Also the parallel notion of man's obligations to God, of man's fidelity, was much in evidence. Israel must obey the law; but Israel was *not* faithful; God was.

The concept gradually develops: for the whole history of Israel revolves around this concept of God's *chesed*, His fidelity. This is the one leading theme that illuminates the central meaning of Israel's history. Israel did not obey God's law and, as time went on, a new element entered into the concept of fidelity, *chesed*, namely, an insistence on the favors that God does to Israel, how much He lavishes upon her as proofs of His love. The *inner* attitude, on God's part, that dictates these favors is not fully underscored; it is more what I have done, what I will do "if you will obey."

Finally, as time goes on, the notion of *chesed* becomes both more interiorized and more universalized. God first had to make Israel realize that He had selected this one people, but later on He makes it clear to His prophets, especially Isaiah, that the love He explicitates to Israel belongs not only to Israel but to *all* people and to *each* individual.

There is also a tremendous development in the interiorization of love in the prophet Hosea. Few of us would have chosen the example that God chose, in the prophet Hosea, to being home God's idea of *chesed*, "faithful love." In Hosea, God chooses to represent Himself. Hosea's wife is a prostitute. One can imagine the anguish, the suffering, the tragedy that Hosea endured. The Lord God Himself, in full understanding of what He was doing, chose Hosea and his prostitute-wife to represent God's constancy and His fidelity to us. He ordered Hosea to search out his wife continuously, to bring home to Israel and us that whatever our infidelity to God, His fidelity is the same as that of the sorrowing, suffering, anguished, loving husband, Hosea. God dares to choose this husband as a figure of Himself—the eternal God. That should cause the Christian and the religious some reflection. The major prophets emphasize especially the fidelity of God in times of suffering and disaster for Israel; it is precisely when everything looks worst for Israel that the prophets insist most strongly upon this theme of *chesed*. God *cannot* abandon his people: the concept is unthinkable; no more can He abandon the individual Christian or religious. No matter what Israel has done, no matter what her circumstances are, God cannot abandon her; and the prophets insist, in the face of all opposition, that He cannot and will not. He shows his faithful love. Hosea, again, underscores to us the completely *gratuitous* nature of the faithful love of God; it has nothing to do with our merits. We Christians and religious love people because they are lovable. Not so with God, who does not love us because we are lovable, but makes us lovable, that He may love us more.

Hosea insists that God's love is totally self-motivated: it flows out of the depths of His own being. It does not arise from the fact that we have obeyed the law, or have been faithful to Him, as docile, obedient servants. God's faithful love is not a response to values that exist in sinless man; rather, it *creates* values in man. By insisting upon this notion, Hosea transfers the notion of fidelity from the covenantal, legal notion to the deeply personal concept of a spousal-love between God and the individual. Jeremiah stresses more the father-son relationship. Whenever the fidelity of God is stressed in the analogue of father to son, it is interesting to note the warmth and *forgiveness.* God's love is not the delight of a father in his upstanding son; rather, whenever the note of fidelity is stressed in the father-son relationship, it is always this: "My son is so fragile; my son could so easily abandon me; my son could so easily be unfaithful." It is the notion of *compassionate* fidelity. In the some ten places where Israel is called *son,* the context is always one of a deep compassion for the weakness of God's son, whom He loves despite his weakness.

This notion of *chesed* is also joined to another Hebrew word, *ahab,* a word for love which has a different emphasis from *chesed. Ahab* suggests a completely unconditioned free choice, an election, implying that God moved out, for what reason no one can say, to love this individual. *Ahab,* for example, is never used for parental love or filial love, where there is a motive; "he is my father, he is my son." *Ahab* is used rather for love with feeling, passionate love, but completely unconditioned. It is a word used to express God's relationship to Israel and to men.

We may join to that a third Hebrew word used of God's love. It expresses, if we may use the term, the "mother love" of God. It is derived from a word which has to do with the womb, and connotes the kind of tenderness we associate normally with mother love—the word *rahahmin*.

The central idea of this theme of fidelity is that God's love is stable, loyal, unchanging, faithful. It is a steadfast loyalty. This central theme of God's fidelity should dominate the climate of the Christian's spiritual life.

But what of us—granted that God is faithful, we are not. What of our sins? It is evident in all the scriptural analysis that our sins cannot alter this fidelity of God. He pursues Israel as Hosea pursues his prostitute wife. So He pursues us in our infidelity. Over and over Israel, and the Christian, the religious, are unfaithful. This does not release God from His vows of fidelity.

But does not a Christian life have a certain tension? Are we not told that the fear of God is the beginning of wisdom? Do we not fear God? Should we not fear God? Our Christian life must have a unity to it. We cannot fear God one day and stand in utter trust of Him the following day. We cannot accept that psychological alternation. How can we divide God? Is He not the same today as yesterday? If I am unfaithful today, does God change? Do I divide my own approach to God? How can I preserve psychological unity? But Abraham feared God, Isaiah feared God, Moses feared God, and Peter feared God. True, but we certainly cannot fear God as a tyrant; that is injurious to the meaning of God. We fear our own unfaithfulness. What the Scriptures call "fear" of God we would not cover by the same word. When the Scriptures tells us to fear God, they attach to the word *fear* a meaning different from the ordinary. We must *fear* to offend someone we love deeply. It is not a *fear* in our sense at all, but it is a "fear" to alter a delicate love-relationship. In human life we can rupture a friendship. If I offend men often enough and persistently enough, their capacity for forgiveness may disappear. God's forgiveness is infinite. Even our sins, as Augustine says, are used by God to integrate us into a more totally complete love-relationship with Him. The Christian is more marvelously remade after sin and repentance. This is literally, theologically true. Man is not less graced after sin and repentance; he is more graced. Weak human beings wear out their capacity for forgiveness. God's capacity to forgive is infinite. After all the sins of the world, His capacity for fidelity is utterly undiminished. How could it be diminished? It is infinite.

If men wish to think of their infidelity in terms of God's fidelity, they should think of a momentary lover's quarrel. We Christians are like children, occasionally bad, but few managing to combine great malice of intention with great objective evil. We must integrate our concept of sin with that of God's fidelity by realizing that the individual sinful acts that we perform are not a complete disaster. If one carefully examines an impressionistic portrait, he will see little dots of red or black in a great masterpiece. Put under a microscope, they would be ugly, but when one sees the whole portrait as a totality, it is a masterpiece. So with the sincere Christian—his little sins, little defects, big sins, big defects are dots here and there on his moral portrait. What counts is the entire portrait, and this takes the Christian, and the religious, a lifetime to finish. We will finish it perfectly only in that instant of death which we call purgatory, where we experience an instantaneous stretching in love and fully finish the portrait.

God's forgiveness is not merely a legal procedure. He does not give a legal declaration: "this is over and done with." God grants man, in forgiving him through His fidelity, the grace to recreate himself interiorly. "Surely there are things that really offend?" "Yes." Let us look at it from the point of view of the Scriptures: what offends God especially is lack of faith, lack of belief in God's fidelity to us, lack of trust in Him, and hard-heartedness, to be as St. Paul said, "without affection," without love.

There is only one natural and proper response to God's faithful love, and that is the same faithful, trusting love of Him and the neighbor. There is no point in saying that one loves the invisible God whom he does not see, if he does not love our visible neighbor, the sacrament of God. The normal response to God's steadfast-loyalty to us is the same steadfast-loyalty to Him and to our neighbor.

Religious should reflect on this: throughout Sacred Scripture, when the word *faithfulness* or *fidelity* is applied to a person, it is not applied to men. It is applied to God. It is not upon man that Scripture lays the emphasis for fidelity, though it does that too. Primarily, when Sacred Scripture talks about faithfulness, it is referring to one Person, the eternal God in His relationship to man.

Whatever problems confront religious life today, the Lord is faithful. Religious have given public, corporate, faithful witness to the eschatological kingdom of the Lord. And the Lord is faithful. *Sicut erat in principio et nunc et semper et in aeternum.*